W9-CJW-833

# The Secret of Shakespeare's Doublet

Fr. Bacon

# The Secret of Shakespeare's Doublet

by Jane W. Beckett

Peter E. Randall, Publisher

*Printed in the United States of America*

*Peter E. Randall, Publisher*
*36 Mace Road*
*Hampton, N.H. 03842*

**Library of Congress Cataloging in Publication Data**

Beckett, Jane W                    1902-1977.
The secret of Shakespeare's doublet.

Bibliography: p.
Includes index.
1. Shakespeare, William, 1564-1616--Authorship--Baconian theory. 2. Bacon, Francis, Viscount St. Albans, 1561-1626--Cipher. 3. Authors, English--Early modern, 1500-1700--Biography. I. Title.
PR2944.B36 1977    822.3'3    77-21291

"The name 'William Shakespeare' is most probably a pseudonym behind which there lies concealed a great unknown".

Sigmund Freud

## *Contents*

# *Illustrations*

## *Foreword*

THE attribution of Shakespeare's Plays to the strolling actor from Stratford-on-Avon whose name they bear must be one of the more successful hoaxes ever put over on the reading and theater-going public. When I was introduced to them in my high school days, for instance, I don't remember that any question was ever raised about their authorship; and when, from time to time subsequently, I happened to hear or read that it was disputed, my ignorance and early conditioning tended to make me disregard such voices. Not until I happened to be asked to read the manuscript of *The Secret of Shakespeare's Doublet* did it finally dawn on me that there might be something "rotten in the state of Denmark" with respect to the Shakespeare authorship.

Mrs. Beckett disposes of Shakespeare's claim to authorship (if it can be called that, since he apparently never himself expressed any awareness of it) by quoting all the known facts of his life, not one of which relates him to the literary masterpieces that have made his name famous. She supports the belief shared by many others that their creator was Francis Bacon and that Shakespeare was merely a nom de plume which Bacon used for political and personal reasons. The clue which indirectly led to her discovery of what she regards as a deliberate attempt on the part of Bacon to leave his "concealed signature" on the title pages of Shakespeare's works derives from the portrait of Shakespeare in the celebrated 1623 First Folio of his plays. The portrait shows him garbed in a strangely designed coat, or doublet, as the Elizabethans called it. Closer examination of the garment reveals, as

Mrs. Beckett points out, quoting the "Gentleman's Tailor Magazine" for April, 1911, that "the righthand side of the forepart is obviously the lefthand side of the backpart; and so give a harlequin appearance to the figure, which it is not unnatural to assume was intentional, and done with express object and purpose."

In 1923, three centuries after the publication of the First Folio, W. H.M. Grimshaw, commenting on the doublet in Shakespeare's portrait, suggests that its curious cut may be intended as a pun on the word doublet. "Double it; double what?" Mrs. Beckett imagines Grimshaw asking himself, and continues, "He applied this doubling idea to the text of the poem by Ben Jonson which faces the Shakespeare portrait. First he wrote the poem forwards and left a space between each letter for a second writing. He then *doubled-it* by writing the poem backwards in the empty spaces. To his great surprise the doubled text revealed the name BACON."

Following Mr. Grimshaw's lead, Mrs. Beckett decided to apply the doublet method of writing a text forwards and backwards to the title page of the 1623 First Folio. Obtaining a facsimile copy of this from the Rare Books Department of the New York Public Library and "a sheet of architect's paper with five squares to the inch," she set to work. The procedure, described and illustrated in detail in her book, also disclosed the name BACON. The same happened when she continued the experiment with the title pages of the first quarto editions of the individual Shakespeare plays and the title page of the *Sonnets*. In each instance she came upon the concealed "signature" BACON, sometimes alone, sometimes together with FRANCIS, F, FR, or FRA, and occasionally with the words WRIT (WRITER), POET, or KTC (abbreviation of knight) added.

At this point it may be natural to ask: Why was Bacon unwilling to disclose himself as author of his poetic works and at the same time saw to it that his name was identified with them? This and many other questions prompted by the continuing mystery surrounding the authorship of Shakespeare's works, and especially insofar as Bacon's relation to this authorship is concerned, the reader will find interestingly discussed and documented in *The Secret of Shakespeare's Doublet.*

Halfdan Gregersen
Former Professor, Romance Languages
Harvard College
Former Dean,
Williams College

Jane W. Beckett

## *Author's Preface*

PERHAPS the story of my interest in the Bacon-Shakespeare controversy should begin when I was seven years old. I had already seen several of the finest actors in the great Shakespearian plays and so, when I visited Stratford-on-Avon, England, with my parents and sister I had, even at that early age, some idea of who Shakespeare was and what he had written. I remember the Church of the Holy Trinity where Shakespeare was buried. I was impressed by the exquisite stained glass windows, which cast jewelled lights on the cold gray stones of the floor and walls. And I remember my father's voice, as he read the inscription on the tombstone as it appears today:

We wondered at this strange verse which seemed so out of place on the tombstone of the great William Shakespeare.

In the birthplace of Shakespeare we were shown the dark cellar and the hooks where the butcher's assistant, young William Shakespeare, hung the meat and the vessels which he used for his repulsive tasks. It was with a sigh of relief that I emerged into the bright sunshine again. Perhaps my little face showed the disgust and disappointment which I felt so keenly. At any rate my father took me by the hand and led me away from the crowd. There, among the beautiful flowers of Ann Hathaway's garden, he told me that many people did not believe that William Shakespeare of Stratford-on-Avon wrote the plays but that he was only a living mask for the great philosopher and Lord Chancellor, Francis Bacon. I can still remember the chills that ran through me at this story and the conviction that came over me that it was true.

At nineteen I married Wheeler Beckett, a young musician, who was the organist and Choir Master of Grace Cathedral San Francisco, and from that time on my life was devoted to him, to his dreams as a composer and to his work as an orchestral conductor. Our life was filled to the brim with activity, rushing off to Europe from San Francisco, after his season's work ended, to study conducting with Felix Weingartner in Basel, Switzerland. Then back to California for more work. This continued for a number of years. In time my husband became the conductor of the Richmond Symphony Orchestra in Virginia, the Boston Symphony Orchestra Youth Concerts in Boston and, for thirty two consecutive years, the New York Youth Concerts in Carnegie Hall and Philharmonic Hall at Lincoln Center. This last activity made it necessary for us to find a home near by and we settled in Englewood, New Jersey.

Our next door neighbor was Frederick S. Duncan, patent attorney for the American Chain and Cable Company. He was also the founder of the Shakespeare Club in Englewood, a group of enthusiastic Shakespearians who met weekly to read the plays. A marble bust of Shakespeare stood in one corner of Mr. and Mrs. Duncan's livingroom. He accepted, as most people do, William Shakespeare as the true author of the plays. We had not been living in Englewood very long, however, before something happened which caused him to have his first doubts. I showed him a book which I had just received from England. Its title was, "The Secret History of Francis Bacon — (our Shakespeare)" by Alfred Dodd. This book gave a new interpretation and arrangement of the Sonnets and it also contained examples of the simple, the reverse and the Kay numerical ciphers. This was my introduction to the world of ciphers, and it opened the field of Elizabethan literature to me. I began to search for numerical ciphers in the books of the period of Francis Bacon, including his acknowledged works and those of Shakespeare. I was struck by the similarity of the numerical signatures which I found in these works. It did not seem to me to be possible that they could be there without intention and design.

I read Francis Bacon's essay on ciphers and I learned that he worked for Queen Elizabeth and Essex in this field. I read of his invention of the biliteral cipher, that ingenious method of concealing a message by using two fonts of type. I tried my hand at deciphering a message in the biliteral cipher, and after many weeks of work, I triumphantly took my findings to a new friend, Professor George Curtis of Lehigh University, Bethlehem, Penn. Professor Curtis had done a great deal of work in this field and was a Baconian. With pride I presented him with my "great discovery." To my surprise he leaned back in his chair with a hearty laugh and said, "If you had been making your living as a professional cipherist, as I did for a number of years, you would know that once you start you have to continue straight through to the end of a message without any shifting around, as you have done here to make your point." This was my first lesson and I never forgot it. But it was such a shock that my enthusiasm for my own work in deciphering was considerably dampened. More than two years went by before I took this work up again.

In the meantime I became interested in the work that Professor George Curtis had done. He had a wonderful collection of books and had prepared slides showing the minute differences in the two fonts of type used in the biliteral cipher of Francis Bacon. He was kind enough to lend me several of his books and although I only saw him three or four times before his untimely death, I learned a great deal from him.

My own library was beginning to grow. Mr. Duncan gave me a facsimile of the 1623 First Folio, the first printed collection of all the Shakespeare plays. He also gave me facsimiles of the first and second quartos of Hamlet, Henry IV, Venus and Adonis, The Passionate Pilgrim, the Sonnets, Lucrece, Pericles and Titus Andronicus. Through a book dealer, he learned of a collection of books on the Bacon-Shakespeare controversy. My husband bought this collection for me. I began to go through it to see what other persons had done in an attempt to solve the many perplexing questions of this fascinating subject. I read Mrs. E. W. Gallop's *Bi-Literal Cypher of Francis Bacon;* also her *Lost Manuscripts;* Sir Edwin Dunning Lawrence's *Bacon is Shakespeare* and William Stone Booth's *Some Acrostic Signatures of Francis Bacon.* There was *Bacon's Promus* by Mrs. Henry Pott. Altogether there were 66 books and a whole stack of the British magazine, *Baconiana.*

In the June 1923 issue of *Baconiana,* there was an article by W. H. M. Grimshaw entitled, *Droeshout's Frontispiece, 1623, and Verses to the Reader. In the First Folio of William Shakespeare, with a Note on the 46th Psalm.* It contained a very interesting arrangement of the text of the poem, *To The Reader* by Ben Johnson. In his article, Mr. Grimshaw shows how the name BACON can be found in this poem.

(Editor's note: Grimshaw's method and Mrs. Beckett's adaptation of it are fully described in Chapter one. She began this aspect of her work in the early 1950's and for the next 25 years, she was rarely without sheets of architect's paper as she experimented with the title pages of the anonymous plays, the title page of the 1623 First Folio, the sonnets and the tombstone that lies on the floor of the chancel of the Church of the Holy Trinity in Stratford-on-Avon.

In every case, she found not only the word *Bacon* but other significant words as well, as explained in the text. The presence of these unsought words reduces to an astronomical figure the likelihood of coincidence.

Jane Beckett died on March 6, 1977, before the final details of her work had been completed. We have edited this manuscript for publication with the assistance of her husband, Wheeler.

Jane Beckett did not seek to destroy the value of the writings attributed to Shakespeare, but she did want to show how such works could not have been produced by a person with the limited background of the man from Stratford-on-Avon. It was her hope that this book would convince others to begin independent and objective research into the true authorship of the works attributed to William Shakespeare.

Jane Beckett knew that many other people have been suggested as the true author and she sets forth in the written portion of this book her reasons why she believed only Francis Bacon had all of the qualifications for authorship as well as the means to pay for the publishing of the plays, sonnets and other works.)

## *Some Aspects of the Bacon-Shakespeare Controversy*

THIS subject, which has been the cause of much anger and vituperation among scholars and laymen alike, is one that should be approached with the spirit of adventure and openmindedness which must have possessed those amazing men who sought and found the great New World of the Americas. Perhaps this might be put in another way by quoting Francis Bacon's own words, "Read not to contradict and confute, nor to believe and take for granted, nor to find talk and discourse, but to weigh and consider."

The first doubts, expressed in print, concerning the Shakespearean authorship, were published in 1597 in a volume of satires by Joseph, afterwards Bishop Hall. One of the writers lampooned, who was clearly identified as the author of *Venus and Adonis* of 1593 was named "Labeo". In 1598, John Marston, in his *Pigmalion's Image*, took Hall to task over his indictment of some of these authors and, in particular, of "Labeo", whom Marston associated with the words "Mediocria Firma" which were, of course, the Bacon heraldic motto. There is no mistaking this obvious clue which, like many other contemporary pieces of evidence, is ignored by the orthodox critic. The year 1598 also witnessed the publication of the first play quarto on which was printed, as author, the name Shakespeare (or "Shake-Speare") and, in the year following, doubts were expressed in no uncertain terms about this apparent imposture, but more of this later.

At intervals between the beginning of the seventeenth and the middle of the eighteenth centuries, many important references to Bacon's extensive concealed authorship were published. Among these was Dr. Thomas Tenison's *Baconiana* of 1679 which contained many hints of this nature, including the words, "And those who have true skill in the Works of Lord Verulam, like great Masters in Painting, can tell by the Design, the Strength, the way of colouring, whether he was the author of this or the other Piece, though his name be not to it." In 1769, the year that David Garrick organized the first celebrations at Stratford to honour its famous son, a curious little book, attributed to a Dr. Herbert Lawrence, was published with the title *The Life and Adventures of Common Sense.* A character, "Wisdom", who can clearly be identified with Francis Bacon, complains that his Common Place Book, containing rules and notes on every subject useful for dramatic writing, had been stolen by a person belonging to the Playhouse whose name was Shakespeare and who commenced playwriting. This was followed in 1786 by the anonymous *The Story of the Learned Pig* which is now thought to have been written by the Rev. J. Wilmot, a Baconian scholar who lived at Barton-on-the Heath, near Stratford-on-Avon. This erudite and amiable pig assures us that amongst his many amusing adventures, he encountered a Player who stole some of his writings and published them as his own. These writings are named as five of the Shakespeare plays. Later, in 1848, Mr. Joseph Hart, American Consul at Santa Cruz, Canary Islands, published, in an article called *The Romance of Yachting,* his convictions that the money-loving actor could not be the author of the plays.

It was not, however, until 1857 when scholars were discovering that the Shakespeare works were replete with expert knowledge of many abstruse subjects like classical history, Greek mythology, law, medicine, foreign languages and travel etc., that the controversy really got under way. In that year, the gifted American, Delia Bacon, and the Englishman, William H. Smith, simultaneously published books, which, from two different points of view, argued that Francis Bacon was the true author of the plays and poems. These books were treated with derision and contempt. In 1867 James Spedding started to publish his researches on Bacon and the public became aware of this man's real character, his wit, his integrity, his literary ambitions and his great love of humanity. Spedding, however, was not attracted to the idea that Bacon wrote the Shakespeare plays. Later, the Barrister, Hepworth Dixon, in his biography of Bacon, was able to prove conclusively that his fall from the office of Lord Chancellor was a political manoeuvre by unscrupulous men. In 1885, The Bacon Society was founded in England by Mrs. Henry Pott who gathered around her a coterie of writers and others interested in this subject. She was able to study, in the British Museum, Bacon's MS collection of apt sayings, turns of speech, proverbs etc. jotted down for future use. Few of these are to be found in the prose works, but Mrs. Pott found that a great number were used, either verbatim or in poetic language, in the Shakespeare plays. The collection is known as Bacon's *Promus* or Storehouse, and is a valuable witness in favour of the "Bacon theory."

At about this time, scholars like the German, Edwin Bormann, the Englishman W.F.C. Wigston, and the American's H.J. Ruggles and Nathaniel Holmes, independently came to the conclusion that it was Shakespeare's *Comedies, Histories and Tragedies* which formed the last three parts of Bacon's *Great*

*Instauration.* In one of his works, Bacon speaks of "the legitimate method of handing on or commending knowledge" and then says that since men's minds are blocked with misleading "idols" (that is, preconceived notions and errors), he proposes to adopt a new method of insinuating knowledge and wisdom into minds most darkened. This method, he explained, is designed, not only to humour the sick (that is, those "blocked minds") and to attract confidence, but also to reform without dispute or contention, and to spread his philosophy like a vigorous and thriving plant. Bacon's great hope was to reconstruct human knowledge and to restore to man his dominion over nature to the limits of human possibility. This indirect method of teaching painlessly is held by Baconians to be the ultimate purpose of the Shakespeare plays, which are not only a treasurehouse of art, knowledge and wisdom, but which "hold the mirror up to nature" and show men their weaknesses and their strength while, at the same time, pointing to a more fulfilled life by the control and restraint of selfish and unbridled passions. Bacon's views on poetry, which he described as "the second leading branch of learning," give an important back-up to this theory. "Thus poetry not only delights, but inculcates morality and nobleness of soul, whence it may be justly esteemed of divine nature." Bacon then deplores the corruption of the theatre in his day and the neglect of its power for instruction and improving. It was not so with the ancients who made it a vehicle for "improving men in virtue". "Wise men," he said, "and great philosophers, have thought it to be the plectrum of the mind, or as the bow to the violin. For it is a secret of nature that men are more open to impressions congregate (or in company) than when alone." It is interesting, in view of Bacon's remarks on the ancients, that Aristophenes did not have his plays published or produced in his own name, but in the names of his actor-managers. There are many strong reasons why Bacon did not wish to be known as a poet, and above all a dramatic poet, in his life-time or for some time to come, but probably the strongest reason was that this was an essential part of his concealed method of teaching. In his wonderful prayer, which Addison said was more like the devotion of an angel than of a man, Bacon states, "I have, though in a despised weed (that is, a cloak or motley) procured the good of all men."

Space does not permit the mention here of much of the contemporary evidence which gives support to our claims. Subjects such as the similarity of thought and unusual phrases to be found in abundance in the plays and Bacon's prose works, the close study of the meaningful head and tail-pieces to be found in the early 17th century literature which suggests the existence of a silent literary Brotherhood dedicated to the construction of an English language and heritage, Bacon's use of and adaption of the Emblem Literature which was intended to sharpen men's minds to certain truths and which included revelations concerning his "Shakespeare" mask, these things must be passed over. There are, however, some items which must be mentioned.

In 1626, Bacon's former Chaplain, William Rawley, published a collection of thirty-two Latin tributes to his late master by men of letters and men of the Universities and Inns of Court. Twenty-seven of these speak movingly of Bacon as a supreme poet. The collection, now known as the *Manes Verulamiani* (the Shade of Verulam) and now in the British Museum, has been translated but, regretfully, it is ignored by scholars. One of these elegies (number 20) refers to Bacon as "the tenth Muse and the Glory of the choir" while another (number 9) speaks of him as "the precious gem of concealed literature." One writer, in tribute number 4, makes this startling statement, "Just as Eurydice, wandering in the shades of Dis+, yearned to lay hold of Orpheus, and Orpheus, with winged hand, touched the strings of his lyre, so did Philosophy seek Bacon as her champion — and, as she humbly crept in comedy, he did not, after the manner of triflers, patch her but completely renovated her and afterwards, more brilliantly still, in the loftier flight of tragedy he soared, and Aristotle, alive again, flourishes anew in the *Novum Organon*."

Finally, it should be recorded that one writer, the poet Thomas Randolph, tells us in the last poem, "the warmth of his generous heart could no longer, O Goddess Minerva, endure that you should be contemned. His divine pen restored your due honours and this other Apollo dispelled your clouds." Minerva or Pallas Athene, was, of course, the goddess of Wisdom and of the Arts and Science. Her statute in Athens showed her with a forty foot spear which she shook at Ignorance while her helmet was intended to denote invisibility which she employed to do her work. She was, in fact, a "Shake-speare."

We have another important witness for the "Bacon theory" and this is the contemporary playwright, Ben Jonson, whose famous swipe at the actor Shakspere, in his *Every Man out of His Humour* has produced some embarrassment in the Stratford dovecot. This play first appeared in 1599, soon after Shakspere had acquired a coat of arms. Evidently this angered "Honest Ben" and he therefore made a savage attack on his acquaintance in this play. We are introduced to a countryman, ambitious to become a gentleman, who is able to purchase a coat of arms which he shows to some friends. Asked about the crest, he says, "It is your boar, without a head rampant." One character comments sarcastically, "Most apt, a swine without head, brain, wit, anything indeed, ramping to gentility." Another adds, "Let the word be, 'Not without mustard'; your crest is very rare, Sir." (Shakespere's motto was 'Non sans droit'). It would be difficult to find a clearer reference to the ignorant Shakspere and to Bacon, whose crest was a boar, and who was the provider of the missing head.

In 1616, the year that the actor died, this play was reprinted in a folio edition of Jonson's plays. In a later scene, the uncouth countryman, who became a source of considerable amusement to his gentlemen friends, is persuaded to court the vain and fashionable lady, Saviolina. They prepare her for this meeting, telling her she is to meet a rare and charming gentleman whose eloquence and wit will astonish her. This description, which is not unlike a contemporary description of Francis Bacon, is so printed that the initial letters of each line of this speech read, P O E T C A N B O, and this is the gentleman whom the witless Shakspere has been chosen to impersonate! Ben Jonson's attitude towards Bacon seems to have altered considerably between the 1590's and 1620. In 1598, he somehow became aware of the true authorship of the Shakespeare plays of whose style and construction he was highly critical. In the early 1620's he was employed by Bacon, in whose house he resided, ostensibly to help translate some of his prose works into Latin, an occupation he touched on with ironic humour in his *Princes Masque or Time Vindicated,* which was produced at Court in early 1624 just a few months after the publication of the Shakespeare Folio, which he is now thought to have edited. The Masque appears to concern this publication and a boastful, and ridiculous character, Chronomastix, is introduced, "his forehead tip't with bayes," and is acclaimed by the common people as their poet hero. He is carried off in triumph, while Fame, who scorns this imposter says, "I envie not the apotheosis, t'will prove but deifying of a Pompion." (pumpkin) At about this time, Jonson recorded his admiration for Bacon's high moral character and for his literary achievements which he called "the mark or acme of our language."

It is earnestly hoped that some of the Baconian evidence included in his short history of the Controversy, will not receive the same treatment but will be "weighed and considered."

T.D. Bokenham
Surrey, England

Mr. WILLIAM

SHAKESPEARES

COMEDIES,
HISTORIES, &
TRAGEDIES.

Publiſhed according to the True Originall Copies.

LONDON

Printed by Iſaac Iaggard, and Ed. Blount. 1623.

Fig. 1 Title page of the First Folio, 1623.

## *The Secret of Shakespeare's Doublet*

HE portrait of William Shakespeare in the famous 1623 First Folio suggests a mystery. This has to do with the peculiar drawing of the coat, or *doublet,* as it was called in Elizabethan times. The cut of the coat aroused so much comment that the tailors of England were requested to express their opinion on it. Let us see what the *Gentlemen's Tailor Magazine* for April, 1911, has to say.

"It is passing strange that something like three centuries should have been allowed to elapse before the tailor's handiwork should have been appealed to in this particular manner.

"The special point is that in what is known as the authentic portrait of William Shakespeare, which appears in the celebrated First Folio edition, a remarkable sartorial puzzle exists. (fig. 1)

"The tunic, coat, or whatever the garment may have been called at the time, is so strangely illustrated that the right hand-side of the forepart is obviously the left-hand side of the backpart, and so give a harlequin appearance to the figure, which it is not unnatural to assume was intentional and done with express object and purpose."

This remarkable statement completely confirms what the *Tailor and Cutter* newspaper had said on March 9, 1911, namely that the figure put for Shakespeare in the 1623 First Folio was undoubtedly clothed in an impossible coat composed of the back and the front of the same left arm.

Since the artist, Martin Droeshout, was perfectly capable of drawing a coat correctly, one must conclude that he was required to draw the picture according to specific instructions given by someone directing the publication of the First Folio.

W.H.M. Grimshaw was the first to point out that the word doublet might be a pun 'double-it.' Double what? He applied this doubling idea to the text of the poem by Ben Jonson which faces the Shakespeare portrait. First he wrote the poem 'frontwards,' leaving a space between each letter for a second writing. He then 'doubled-it' by writing the poem 'backwards', that is, from right to left, beginning in the first empty space in the lower right hand corner and ending at the upper left. To his great surprise the double text revealed the name *Bacon*. Grimshaw had also pointed out in his article[1] that since the cut of the garment shown in the portrait of Shakespeare in the 1623 First Folio was, as the tailors declared, the back and the front of the same left arm, the words *back front,* used as an anagram, became *Fr. Bacon, Kt.* (knight). Francis Bacon had been knighted in 1603, long before the publication of the First Folio.

Due to the extreme prejudice of the aristocratic world of that period toward the theatre and the writing of plays for the public stage, an assumed name had to be used by a young aristocrat and lawyer who wished to rise as a statesman in the Queen's service.

An obscure actor from Stratford-on-Avon, William Shaksper was used as a convenient, living mask. Was it only by coincidence that this man was selected, or was it because his name has a close similarity with one of the inseparable qualities always associated with Bacon's Muse, Pallas Athene, "The Shaker of the Spear"?

In support of these views contemporary documents are submitted showing that a few keen literary minds of the period, including Ben Jonson, penetrated the concealment, and by covert allusions, attributed the Shakespeare works to Francis Bacon.

With respect to the mechanics of the implanting of a concealed name in many of these works, we turn to Bacon's prose writings.

In *De Augmentis* he makes it clear[2] that he is not only familiar with cyphers and other forms of concealed writings but that he was, himself, the inventor of a biliteral cypher which involved the combining of two complete alphabets, in which both the upper and lower case letters differed only very slightly. His correspondence shows that he made use of cyphers in letters to his mother and to his brother Anthony Bacon, who was assigned to the secret service for Queen Elizabeth on the Continent.

Since Bacon had described, in Latin, in his *De Augmentis,* a method of concealing a message by the use of two nearly identical alphabets he could hardly be expected to use this particular cypher in matters of the greatest importance, namely the concealment of his name for posterity as the true author of the Plays and Sonnets. Therefore, to accomplish this he used a new method, one never described by him either in Latin or in English. It was again a 'double', not a double alphabet but a double writing of a text, first frontwards then backwards, hinted at by the cut of the coat in the famous 1623 First Folio. Before using this method of concealment on the title page

# To the Reader.

This Figure, that thou here ſeeſt put,
It was for gentle Shakeſpeare cut;
Wherein the Grauer had a ſtrife
with Nature, to out-doo the life :
O, could he but haue drawne his wit
As well in braſſe, as he hath hit
His face ; the Print would then ſurpaſſe
All, that vvas euer vvrit in braſſe.
But, ſince he cannot, Reader, looke
Not on his Picture, but his Booke.

B. I.

Fig. 2 Ben Jonson's poem, *To The Reader,* First Folio.

of the 1623 First Folio I discovered that Francis Bacon had employed it on the title pages of all the First Quartos (editions) of the Plays, and on the Sonnets as well.

So simple was this method that it was overlooked and remained a secret for some 300 years until Grimshaw discovered it in 1923. Grimshaw, however, never used this method of concealing the name of Bacon in any of the Shakespeare works, but only in the poem, "To the Reader" by Ben Jonson on the first page of the 1623 First Folio.

So unusual was this method of double writing that when I first came upon it in an old copy of *Baconiana* I felt certain that it must be a clue to the authorship of something much greater than a poem signed by Ben Jonson's initials and which was merely a gracious introduction to the Folio. (fig. 2)

Upon thinking this over I decided that it would be interesting to find out if the application of the 'front-back' method would bring forth the name *Bacon* if all the letters on the title page of the 1623 First Folio were used. For I reasoned that had Grimshaw found anything there he would have published it. A survey of twenty years of *Baconiana* subsequent to June 1923 failed, however, to show any further writing by Grimshaw or anyone else on this subject.

I felt that there was, logically, a possibility that this unique method of concealment had been used elsewhere and that since it had been found in the poem, "To the Reader" in the First Folio, the next place to look would be on the title page of the Folio itself, since this was to the left of the page containing the Poem.

In the rare books department of the New York Public Library I found an original 1623 First Folio. At my request a facsimile of the title page was made. With this in hand and a sheet of architect's paper with five squares to the inch before me, I proceeded to carefully examine all of the letters on this page.

I decided that the small letters directly under the picture, 'Martin Droeshout Sculpsit London.' and the date, '1623' must also be used, as a part of the text, in their proper sequence. The text would then read as follows:

Mr. VVILLIAM SHAKESPEARES COMEDIES, HISTORIES, & TRAGEDIES. Published according to the

True Originall Copies. Martin Droeshout Sculpsit London. LONDON Printed by Isaac Jaggard, and Ed. Blount. 1623. (fig. 1)

The text contained three *Bs,* six *Cs,* ten *Ns,* twelve *As* and thirteen *Os.* I began by counting the letters and spaces between each word from each *B* to each *C* and then from each *C* to each *N.* I found that the last *N* in the second *London* was seventeen spaces from the *C* in *Isaac,* and the C in *Isaac* was seventeen spaces from the *B* in *Blount.* This gave me the length of my line. Seventeen spaces across would put the *N, C* and *B* under each other. I now drew my chart, starting with the M of *Mr.* in the first square and ending with the number 3 of *1623* in the last one. To my surprise I found my other two letters, *O* and *A,* adjoining my *N* and *C.* This gave the name *Bacon* beginning with the *B* in *Blount.*

Wondering what the Doublet method would produce I doubled my 17 squares to 34. I used a black pencil for the forward writing and a blue pencil for the backwards writing in the additional squares. Again the name *Bacon* appeared. This I wrote in red. The letters *B, C* and *N* were the same as those used in the single, 'frontwards' text, but the *A* and *O* in the double text came from different words; the A from *William* and the O from *Comedies.* (fig. 40)

This unique way of concealing a name is not a cypher, a cryptogram or an anagram. It is an original form of concealment invented by an expert. I wondered if the same method had been used long before on the title pages of the first quartos (editions) of the Shakespeare plays. Eighteen of these had been printed in numerous editions before they were gathered together with eighteen unpublished plays, making thirty-six in all in the 1623 First Folio.



The title pages of the first quartos were so strangely printed[3] that it seemed worthwhile to test them. Moreover the first editions of the first six plays attributed to Shakespeare were printed in quarto without an author's name. This in itself seemed odd.

| First Quarto Edition | | The Author, as shown on the Title Page |
|---|---|---|
| 1594 | Titus Andronicus | Anonymous |
| 1594 | 2 Henry VI | Anonymous |
| 1595 | 3 Henry VI | Anonymous |
| 1597 | Richard II | Anonymous |
| 1597 | Richard III | Anonymous |
| 1597 | Romeo and Juliet | Anonymous |
| 1598 | Love's Labour's Lost | By W. Shakespere |
| 1598 | 1 Henry IV | Anonymous |
| 1600 | 2 Henry IV | Written by William Shakespeare |
| 1600 | Henry V | Anonymous |
| 1600 | A Midsummer Night's Dream | Written by William Shakespeare |
| 1600 | The Merchant of Venice | Written by William Shakespeare |
| 1600 | Much Ado About Nothing | Written by Willaim Shakespeare |
| 1602 | The Merry Wives of Windsor | By William Shakespeare |
| 1603 | Hamlet | By William Shake-speare |
| 1608 | King Lear | By M. William Shak-speare |
| 1609 | Troilus and Cressida | Written William Shakespeare |
| 1622 | Othello | Written by VVilliam Shakespeare |

For my next experiment I chose the title page of the first quarto of the earliest of the Histories, 2 Henry VI, 1594, the second play on the list. I secured a facsimile of the title page from the New York Public Library. This was one of the anonymous plays and the lack of an author's name provided an additional incentive. (fig. 60)

The results proved to be very interesting. The Doublet writing produced *Bacons-Writ* with *FR* as well. I did not at first grasp the significance of the word *writ* until I found it used in King Lear, Act V, Scene 3, "for my writ is on the life of Lear" and in Cymbeline, Act III Scene 7, "is the tenor of the emperor's writ," and again in Titus Andronicus, Act II, Scene 4, "too late I bring the fatal writ." *Writ,* I saw was frequently used to indicate something written by a person.

Using the Doublet method I found this word three more times, together with the name *Bacon,* in the title pages of the first editions of the quartos of the following Histories: 3 Henry VI, 1595; 1 Henry IV, 1598; and 2 Henry IV, 1600. It is interesting to note that in the case of Henry V, 1600, the Doublet method produced something new, not *writ* but *poet* in connection with *Bacon.* (See examples of this and other title pages, figs. 45-61).

## *Documented Evidence on the Life of William Shakespeare of Stratford-on-Avon*

No one in Elizabethan or Jacobean England, the period during which the Plays were created, ever claimed to be their author, certainly not the actor, William Shakesper of Stratford-on-Avon. He never mentioned them in any document, including his will. Nor did his widow, his daughters, their husbands or his grand-daughter, Lady Barnard, claim that he was the author of the plays.

William Shakespere died in 1616 without mentioning in the three pages of his will any Plays, Poems or Sonnets. Nor was there any mention of books, although these were of greater value than some of the minor household effects listed in the will. No letters to printers or producers of plays have ever been found. Yet, at the time of his death, many of the Plays had been on the stage in London for twenty-four years. They had also been given in Germany at the Court of the Duke of Brunswick and in Denmark. Moreover during this period the Shakespeare plays had been printed in various editions (quartos), with new lines added and important changes made. These must have required a correspondence with printers but no scrap of correspondence about any subject in Shakespeare's handwriting has ever been found although scholars have searched diligently, if unsuccessfully, for such evidence.

In fact the lack of factual evidence was so distressing to John Payne Collier, the noted Shakespearian scholar and author of three books on Shakespeare, that, when asked to write a paper for the Shakespeare Society in 1845, he *forged* references to Shakespeare into the Henslowe Diary, which he had borrowed from Dulwich College. These forgeries were exposed in 1881 by Sir George Frederick Warner, Custodian of Manuscripts for Dulwich College. Warner wrote, "A number of forged interpolations have been made (in the Diary) the responsibility for which rests with Collier." Warner's statement cannot be doubted. He later became Custodian of Manuscripts at the British Museum.

Philip Henslowe was the manager of four theatres in London, including the largest, The Fortune. He kept a business diary in which he listed twenty-seven well-known playwrights, whose plays he produced during a period of eighteen years from 1591-2 to 1609. In his diary he wrote the date, the name of the play and the amount paid to the author. In order to keep the record of payments clear Henslowe required each one to sign his name under the entry. These included Ben Jonson, Chapman, Chattle, Day, Dekker, Hathaway, Kyd, Marston, Marlowe, Middleton, Nash, Porter, Rankins, Rowley, Shaa, Wadeson and Webster.

The name of William Shakespeare did not originally appear anywhere in the Diary until John Payne Collier forged it in 1845. Philip Henslowe tells us that he had on various dates, which he lists, produced as a 'new play', *Henry VI,* on March 3, 1591-2; a new play, *Titus Andronicus* on 23 January 1593-4; a new play *Henry V,* on 28 November 1595, as well as three plays which he lists as 'old plays': *King Lear* on 8 April 1594; *The Taming of a Shrew,* 9 June 1594, and *Hamlet* on 11 June 1594.

These six plays were repeated many times thereafter and entries were made accordingly. But no name of an author or payment for them was originally set down in connection with these entries. This certainly suggests an arrangement which differed completely from that made with all the other playwrights.

Another forgery was made in connection with the last signature on Shakespere's will. Sir Edmond Maunde Thompson, a later Custodian of Manuscripts at the British Museum, states that the last three letters of this signature were added later so that some read it *William Shakespeare* but the original read *William Shaksper,* with either a final 'e' or a flourish over the 'r'.

The only evidence we have about the life and activities of William Shakespere of Stratfond-on-Avon consists of fifty-four documented facts. Anything said or written about him beyond these fifty-four items is but surmise and fiction.

If we group these fifty-four documented facts by subject into seven categories we find that ten of them cover such vital statistics as baptisms, marriage, burials and his Will. Nos. 1, 2, 3, 4, 5, 8, 24, 40, 53 and 54.

Eleven others are concerned with real estate ventures: Nos. 12, 26, 27, 34, 35, 36, 38, 39, 43, 48, 49.

Seven more relate to law suits that Shakespere brought against various persons and the Town of Stratford: Nos. 23, 33, 41, 44, 46, 51, 52.

Two others record his troubles with the law: Nos. 10 and 11.

Another pair are accounts of actions he took against the common good: Nos. 14 and 50.

Nine items constitute a miscellany, mostly of minor importance:

Nos. 9, 13, 16, 17, 18, 19, 20, 45, 47.

The remaining thirteen documented facts reflect his preoccupation with the theater, and these *only as an actor:* Nos. 6, 7, 15, 21, 22, 25, 28, 29, 30, 31, 32, 37, 42.

For the benefit of those who would enjoy reading the interesting details of these documented facts and the source of the document, the entire list is presented chronologically, beginning with Shakespere's baptism in 1564 and ending with his burial in 1616 at the age of fifty-three.

*The List of Fifty-Four Documented Facts Constituting all that is Known About the Life of William Shakespere*

1. 1564, April 26: The first record is of his baptism, written in Latin in the Stratford Parish Register of Holy Trinity Church. It reads, "Guiliaemus filius Johannes Shakspere". (William son of John Shakspere).

2. 1582, November 27: A license was granted for the marriage of William Shaksper and Anne Whateley, of Temple Grafton. The next day —

3. 1582, November 28: A bond was entered into by Fulk S Sandells and John Richardson, farmers, of Stratford, by way of security to the Bishop for licensing the marriage of William Shagsper and Anne Hathway, of Stratford. The original documents are preserved in the Worcester Diocesan Registry.

4. 1583, May 26: His daughter, Susanna, was baptized. (Stratford Parish Register).

5. 1585, February 2: His twins, Hamnet and Judith, were baptized. (Stratford Parish Register).

6. 1592, August: Publication of a book by the playwright, Robert Greene, entitled, *A Groats-worth of Wit.* In it Greene speaks of "an upstart Crow, beautified with our feathers, that with his *Tygers heart wrapt in a Players hide,* supposes he is as well able to bombast out a blank verse as the best of you; and being an absolute *Johannes fac totum,* is in his own conceit the onely Shake-scene in a countrie". (Original volume in the British Museum).

7. 1594: His name appeared in the accounts of the Treasurer of the Chamber as follows: "To William Kempe, William Shakespeare and Richard Burbage, servaunts to the Lord Chamberleyne, upon the Councille's warrant dated at Whitehall XVth Marcij 1594, for two severall comedies or enterludes shewed by them before her majestie in Christmas tyme laste part viz St. Stephen's daye and Inocents daye xiijli vjss vijd, and by way of her majesties Reward vjli iiijd, in all xxli. (Public Record Office, identified as Pipe Office, Declared Accounts No. 542, Folio 207b, March 15, 1595).

8. 1596, August 11: His son Hamnet was buried at Stratford. (Stratford Parish Register).

9. 1596: An application was made to the heralds for confirmation of a coat of arms granted to John Shakespeare when he was High Bailiff of Stratford in 1568. This was granted on October 20th. (College of Arms, Vincent MS, Article 23).

10. 1596, Michaelmas Term: A Court order was issued for the arrest of William Shakspere. It is contained in a special set of entries "petitions for sureties of the peace", in the rolls of the Court of the Queen's Bench (Public Records Office, London).

    (Translation from the Latin): England. Be it known that William Shakspere, Francis Langley, Dorothy Soer wife of John Soer, and Anne Lee, for fear of death and so forth. Writ of Attachment issued and directed to the Sheriff of Surrey, returnable the eighteenth of St. Martin.

11. 1597, November 15: He failed to make payment of a subsidy (tax) from the Parish of St. Helen's, Bishop-

gate, London. After three years he was traced to Sussex, on the south bank of the Thames. His name was then transferred to the Residuum Sussex, of the Pipe Roll of the Exchequer and entered under October 6, 1600, so that collection of the tax could be made there, and it was ultimately collected in the liberty of the Clink, a reference to the jail on Clink Street, Southwark, London. (The Exchequer Documents relative to Shakespeare's residence in Southwark, printed by M. S. Guiseppi).

12. 1597: He bought New Place at Stratford-on-Avon for L 60 (about the equivalent today of $2400). (Public Record Office, MS Warwick 39, Elizabeth 1597, Easter 237).
13. 1598, January 12: Wyllyn Wyatt Chamberlin, "Pd to Mr. Shakespere for one load of stone xd" (ten pence).
14. 1598, February 4: He was returned on the rolls of Stratford as the holder (during a famine) of 10 quearters of corn. (Miscellaneous Documents 1, 106, Birthplace Museum, Stratford).
15. 1598: He was mentioned as one of the actors in Ben Jonson's *Every Man In His Humor.* (As given in the 1616 Folio of Ben Jonson's Plays).
16. 1598, October 25: A neighbor, Richard Quiney, wrote a letter to him asking for a loan of L30 on security. (Wheler MS Birthplace Museum, Stratford). Note: This is the only letter that has ever been found addressed to William Shakespeare. There are in existence only three contemporary letters referring to Shakespeare in any way and these are not about literature but about small business matters. The first is dated —
17. 1598, January 24: Master Abraham Sturley writes to a friend in London about Shakespeare lending "some monei on some old yarde land or other Shottri or neare about us." (Misc. Document 1, 135, Birthplace Museum, Stratford). The second letter is dated —
18. 1598, November 4: in which the same Abraham Sturley writes to Richard Quiney stating, "Our countriman Mr. Wm. Shak would procure us monei wc I will like of." (Misc. Doc. above). The third letter, written about this time —
19. 1598-1599: is from Adrian Quiney to his son Richard, in which he says: "yff yow bargen with Wm Sha or recover money therefor, brynge youre money homme." (Misc. Doc. above).

    There exists no contemporary letter from anyone to anyone referring to the Stratford actor as being a poet or in any way connected with literature.
20. 1599: A further application was made to the Heralds for leave to impale the arms of Arden in right of Shakespeare's mother on the coat of arms previously granted. (College of Arms, London; MS R 21, formerly G13). See also No. 29, this list.
21. 1599, Christmas Week: A play, *The Return from Parnassus,* Part II was given at Cambridge by the students of St. John's College. The author is unknown but is thought to be one or more of the students. "Shakespeere", as it is spelled, is mentioned in it. (Rawlinston MMS D, 398, Bodleian Library, Oxford).
22. 1600, Christmas Week: *The Return from Parnassus*

*Part III* was given by the students of St. John's College, Cambridge. Shakespeare's name was also mentioned in this play. (It was printed in two editions and there is a copy of each edition in the Bodleian Library, Oxford and the Huntington Library, California). Note: the first play of the set of three, *Pilgrimage to Parnassus* was also written and acted by the students of St. John's College in Cambridge in 1597 but it does not mention Shakespeare's name.

23. 1600: He sued John Clayton in London for £7 and obtained verdict in his favor.

24. 1601, September 8: His father, 'Mr. John Shakespear', was buried at Stratford-on-Avon. (Stratford Parish Register). William was now entitled to use the Shakespere coat of arms and to put 'esquire' or 'gentleman' after his name, which he did. (Facsimile of the coat of arms).

25. 1602, March 13: John Manningham, a barrister of the middle temple, kept a diary that has been preserved. He put down anything he thought interesting and there is an entry for March 13 concerning a story about the actors Richard Burbage and Shakespere. Burbage, after a performance, was invited by a lady to visit her that night, but Shakespere, learning of this, got there first and when Burbage arrived sent word to him that "William the Conqueror came before Richard II". At the end of this entry Manningham wrote, 'Shakspere's name, William'. (Original Diary, British Museum).

26. 1602, May 11: He bought two parcels of land and a Stratford copyhold[4] to William Shakspere. (Birthplace Museum, Stratford-on-Avon).

Fig. 3 Shakespeare's coat of arms. See documented fact 29.

27. 1602, September 28: A document showing Walter Gelteys transfer of a Stratford copyhold to William Shakspere. (Birthplace Museum, Stratford-on-Avon).

28. 1602, Christmas Week: *The Return from Parnassus Part II* was again produced by the students of St. John's College at Cambridge. The name 'Shakespeere' is mentioned in it. (1606 printed editions, Bodleian and Huntington Libraries).

29. 1602: Ralph Brooke, of the College of Arms, made charges against Sir William Dethick, also of the College of Arms (see Nos. 9, 20 and 24 above). One of these charges involved the granting of arms to

"one Shakespear ye Player". (Ralph Brooke Folger MS 423, 1: as described in *The Shakespeare* Documents by Roland Lewis, p. 432 of Vol. II and fig. 3).

It is not without interest to note that, as late as 1602, the College of Arms listed Shakespeare as "ye Player" and not as an author in spite of the fact the name of William Shakespeare as an author had appeared after the letter of dedication of the two poems *Venus and Adonis* and *The Rape of Lucrece* as early as 1593 and 1594 respectively and also on the title pages of the following plays:

| Name of Play | Date of First Quarto (Edition) |
|---|---|
| Love's Labours Lost | 1598 |
| Midsummer Night's Dream | 1600 |
| The Merchant of Venice | 1600 |
| 2 Henry IV | 1600 |
| Much Ado About Nothing | 1600 |
| Merry Wives of Windsor | 1602 |

| | Name of Author | Date of First Performance |
|---|---|---|
| | by W. Shakespere | 1594-95 |
| Written | by William Shakespeare | 1595-96 |
| Written | by William Shakespeare | 1596-97 |
| Written | by William Shakespeare | 1597-98 |
| Written | by William Shakespeare | 1598-99 |
| | by William Shakespeare | 1599-1600 |

30. 1603: He was listed as one of the actors in *Sejanus,* by Ben Jonson.

31. 1603, May 17: His name appeared in the list of actors who received the new King's license to continue playing. (Public Record Office, London).

32. 1604, March 15: His name appeared in the list of actors who each received 4½ yards of scarlet cloth at the King's cost to provide a uniform for the Royal Procession through London. (Pub. Record Office, L. C. $4/5$, London).

33. 1604: He sued Philip Rogres at Stratford for £1-6s for malt delivered and 2s loan. (Wheler MS, Birthplace Museum, Stratford).

34. 1604: A notation in a Stratford record reads: "William Shakespere Lykewise holdeth one cottage and one garden by estimation a quarter of one acre and payeth rent yearly $ij^{s}$ $vj^{d}$. (About $5.00 in modern currency).

35. 1605, July 24: A bond received from Ralph Huband reads: "To William Shakspre, gentleman". It was a bond for the performance of covenants. (Birthplace Museum, Stratford).

36. 1605, September 6: He purchased a moiety of the tithes of Stratford, Old Stratford, Bishopton and Welcombe for £440. This gave him an income of about £60 per year and the privilege of being buried inside the Parish Church. (Birthplace Museum, Stratford).

37. 1605: He was included among a number of fellow actors in the will of Augustine Phillips, who left each of them a small legacy.

38. 1606: In the "Inventory of Ralph Huband's Lands and Goods", the second line reads, "There was Owinge by Mr. Shakspre xxli".

39. 1606: An auditor's record in Stratford shows Shakspere as a Stratford tithe holder.

40. 1608: His mother, Mary Arden Shakspere, was buried. (Stratford Parish Register).

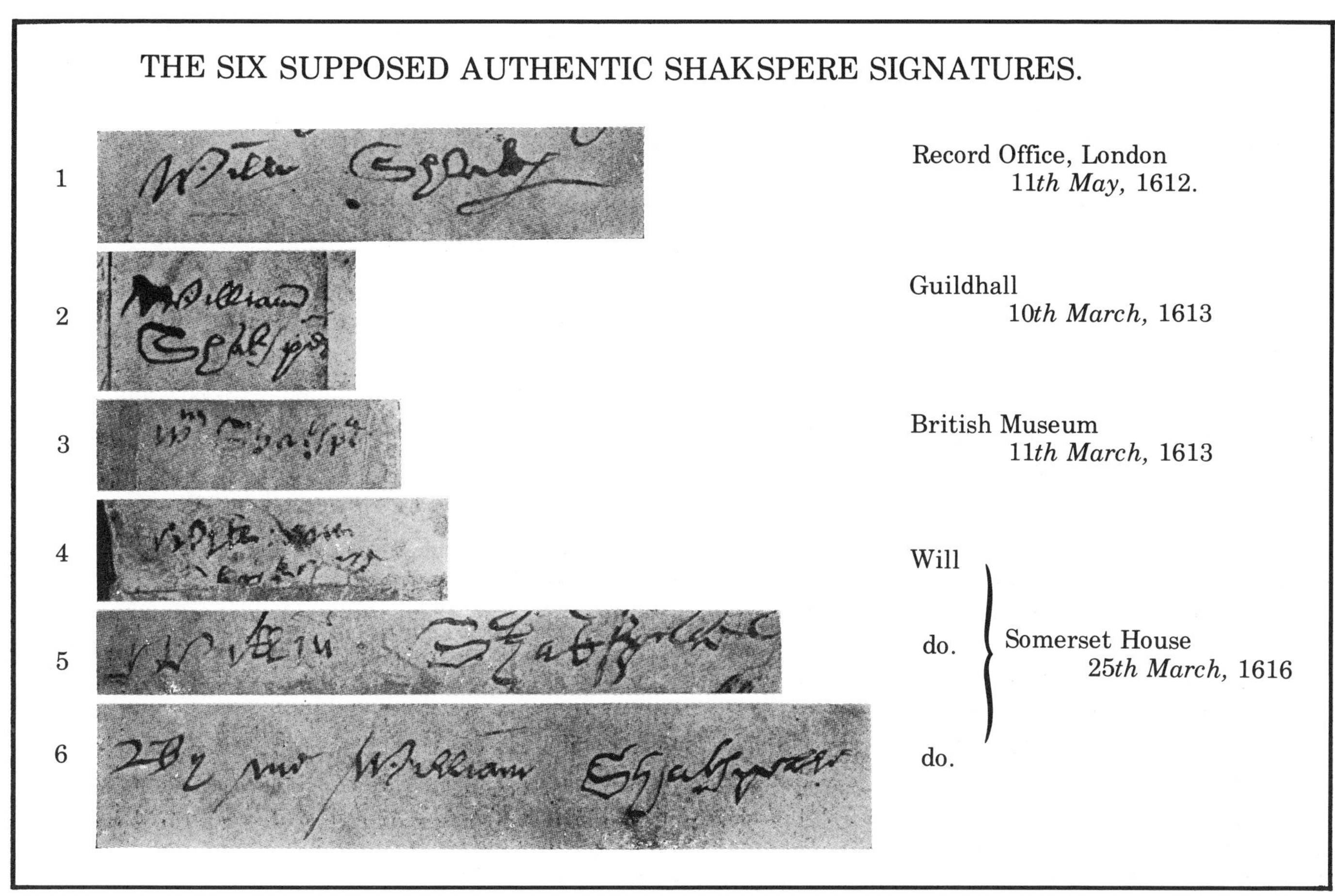


Fig. 4 Six supposed authentic Shakespeare signatures.

41. 1608, August 17: He sued John Addenbroke of Stratford for £6 and obtained judgment with £1-4s for costs. Addenbroke having disappeared he sued his bondsman, Hornby. This suit lasted until June 7, 1609 and involved seven separate documents. (Misc. Documents, Corp. of Stratford).

42. 1608: Ben Jonson's book of plays was printed. In the play *Sejanus* the name, William Shakespeare, is given together with the names of other actors who took part in it.

43. 1611, May 28: He purchased twenty acres of meadow land from John and William Combe at

Stratford for £100. (This Foot of the Fine record is in the Pub. Record Office, London).

44. 1611: He brought suit, with others, to protect his interest in the Stratford tithes. (Draft bill of Complaint respecting tithes, Misc. Documents 11-11, Birthplace Museum, Stratford).

45. 1611, September 11: Shakespere's name was listed, with others, as a contributor to a fund for the promotion of a Bill of Repairs to the Stratford highways. (Misc. Documents, Birthplace Museum, Stratford).

46. 1612, May 11: He signed a deposition in the case of Belot v. Montjoy. (Facsimile of his signature in the Record Office, London, shows "Willn (Blotted) Shaks (blotted) (Fig. 4).

47. 1613, March 31: A record in the household account of the Earl of Rutland lists a payment to Shakespeare and Burbage for their labor in making impress, — heraldic devices on a shield or seal. John Manningham's Diary emphasizes their beauty. B. Roland Lewis says, "That the entry in the household accounts concerns William Shakespeare and not John Shakespeare, the royal bit-maker, is evidenced by his association in this instance with his fellow in the theatre, Richard Burbage."

48. 1613, March 10: He signed a conveyance and purchased a Blackfriars House in London for £140. The signature reads, "W(blotted)illiam Shakspe" with a short flourish over the 'e'. (Facsimile; the original is in the Guild Hall, London).

49. 1613, March 11: He signed a mortgage for the Blackfriars House for £60. The signature reads, "Wm Shakspr" with what might be a small 'a' over the 'r'. (Facsimile; the original is in the British Museum).

50. 1614, October 28: He assisted Thomas Greene in an attempt to enclose the common lands at Stratford, being guaranteed against loss by William Replingham. (Wheler MS., 1, 64, Birthplace Museum. Stratford).

51. 1615, April 26: His name appears in the Bill of Complaints in the suit to recover all the legal documents pertaining to the Blackfriars property.

52. 1615, May 5: The answer of the defendants in the above mentioned suit reads, William Shakespeare, gent."

53. 1616, March 25: He signed his Will on three separate pages. (Facsimile). The original document is preserved at Somerset House, London. It shows that the signatures differ greatly. The first signature appears to be "Willia(blotted)m Shakspere". The second, "Willm (with a short flourish over the 'm') Shakspere, and the third "William Shaksper with either a final 'e' or a flourish after the 'r'. Some read it as "Shakespeare" but the handwriting expert of the British Museum, Sir E. Maunde Thompson, states that the last signature on the Will originally ended by a contraction and that the last three letters were added later. He continues, "The three subscriptions to the Will present difficulties which are almost beyond explanation. They differ from one another to such a degree that it is not going too far to declare that, were they met with on three independent documents, they might not unreasonably be taken, at first sight, for the signatures of three

different persons. And besides their intrinsic dissimilarities, the methods of writing them vary also."

Sir Edmund Kerchever Chambers, whose long article on Shakespeare appears in the 14th Edition of the *Encyclopaedia Britannica,* states that, "No letter or other writing in Shakespeare's hand can be proved to exist, with the exception of the three signatures on his Will, one on a deposition (May 11, 1612), and two upon deeds (March 10 and 11, 1613) in connection with the purchase of his Blackfriars House."

54. 1616, April 23: His burial was recorded in the Parish Register at Stratford-on-Avon as "Will Shakspere", Gent. As a tithe owner he was buried in the Parish Church of the Holy Trinity.

This list of 54 documented facts comprises all that was *written* about the *actor, William Shakspere,* as he spelled it in two places on his will, and as it appeared in the Parish Register.

There is no evidence that he ever attended a local grammar school in Stratford or elsewhere. There is no evidence that he ever attended a college or a University, a law school or worked in a law office.

Yet we are told that he arrived in London with *Venus and Adonis* and *The Rape of Lucrece* in his pocket. These two poems were considered "senseful and exquisite" by the literary censor, Dr. Whitgift, Archbishop of Canterbury, who allowed them to be published.

In 1592 (see No. 6 above) Shakespeare's name was parodied in *A Groats' worth of Wit,* by the playwright, Robert Greene (1558-1592), who wrote about "an upstart crow beautified with our feathers, that with his *Tyger's heart wrapt in a player's hyde* supposes hee is as well able to bombast out a blanke-verse as the best of you; and being an absolute Johannes fac-totum, (Jack of all trades) is in his owne conceyt the onely shake-scene in a countrey". (British Museum).

Who is this "upstart crow beautified with our feathers"? Greene uses 'our' because he has just been writing about a group of playwrights, including himself, Marlowe and Peele. It is clear that Greene is describing an actor, shake-scene, who bedecks himself with author's feathers. The expression, *Tyger's heart wrapt in a player's hyde,* is in Greene's italics because it is a quotation from the anonymous play, 3 Henry VI, Act I Sec. 4, line 137 — *York,* addressing *Queen Margaret,* exclaims, "O tigers heart wrapp'd in a woman's hide"!

If, in 1592, Greene was lampooning the actor, Shakespeare, (shake-scene), it informs us of a valuable fact, not found elsewhere, that the actor was already acting in London by that time. It shows also that Greene knew that this very early historical play was not written by the actor. When the first quarto edition of Henry VI was printed in 1595 no author's name appeared on the title page.

The astute playwright, Robert Greene, had perceived that the anonymous author of this historical play had disguised himself 'in a player's hyde' and was using 'shake-scene', the actor, as a cover for his literary works.

A play entitled *The Return from Parnassas* was produced at Cambridge in 1600 (Nos. 21 and 22 of Documented Facts) and printed anonymously in 1606. It contains some interesting lines that lampoon "Shakespeere" the actor, who made his way from Stratford to London and prospered thereafter. (VII 13-16).

*England* Affords these glorious vagabonds,
That carried earst their fardels on their Backes,
Coursers to ride on through the gazing streetes,
Sooping it in their glaring Satten sutes,
And pages to attend their maisterships:
With mouthing words that better wits have framed
They purchase lands, and now esquires are named.

In 1594 the name "Shakespeare" again appears in print in a different form, "Shake-speare", with a hyphen. This is found in *A tribute to the Poet* in *Willobie His Avisa.* The significance of this hyphen is explained in a later chapter.

*Willobie His Avisa*
Annonymous, 1594

"Though Coloatine have deerly bought
To high renowne, a lasting life,
And found that most in vaine have sought
To have a Faire and Constant Wife,
Yet Tarquyne pluckt his Glistering grape,
And Shake-speare paints poore Lucrece rape".

The allusion is to the poem, *The Rape of Lucrece,* which had no author's name on the title page, although it was accompanied by a letter of dedication to the Earl of Southampton, signed, (in print) William Shakespeare, without the hyphen. The hyphenated form of the name was never used by any member of the Shakespeare family, either in Stratford-on-Avon or in any other part of England. Although there are various spellings of the name, none were ever hyphenated.

There is a pamphlet called "Ratsei's Ghost, or the Second Part of his mad Pranks and Robberies." The pamphlet bears no date but was entered at Stationer's Hall, May 31, 1605. The only copy in existence used to be in Earl Spencer's library at Althorp and is now in the Redlands Library at Manchester. It is reprinted by Halliwell Phillipps in his *Outlines of Shakespeare,* 1889, Vol. I, page 325.

Halliwell Phillipps believed that the reference is unquestionably to William Shakespeare of Stratford. The most important part is spoken by Ratsei the Robber to a country player:

*Ratsei* And for you sirra, saies hee to the chiefest of them, thou hast a good presence upon a stage; methinks thou darkenest thy merite by playing in the country. Get thee to London, for if one man were dead, they will have much neede of such a one as thou art. There would be none in my opinion fitter than thyselfe to play his parts. My conceipt is such of thee, that I durst venture all the mony in my purse on thy head to play Hamlet with him for a wager. There thou shalt learn to be frugall — for players were never so thriftie as they are now about London — and to feed upon all men, to let none feede upon thee; to make thy hand a stranger to thy pocket, thy hart slow to performe what thy tongue promise, and when thou feelest thy purse well lined, buy thee some place of lordship in the country, that growing weary of playing, thy mony may there bring thee to dignitie and reputation: then thou needest care for no man, nor not for them that before made thee prowd with speaking their words upon the stage.

See Documented Evidence, Nos. 12, 24. Here again, as in the case of *The Return from Parnassus* quotation (above), the words spoken by Ratsei "then thou needest

Fig. 5 Book plate of Sir Nicholas Bacon, Francis Bacon's father.

care for no man, nor not for them that before made thee proud with speaking their words upon the stage" indicate that the person addressed was an actor, not an author.

Another reference to Shakespeare, made during his lifetime but not published until 1616, the year of his death, is No. 56 of Ben Jonson's *Epigrams*. We quote from the first nine lines:

> Poor poet ape, that would be thought our chief,
> Whose works are e'en the frippery of wit
> From brokage is become so bold a thief
> As we, the robbed, leave rage and pity it.
> At first he made low shifts, would pick and
> glean,
> Buy the revision of old plays; now grown
> To a little wealth and credit in the scene
> He takes up all, makes each man's wit his own,
> And told of this he slights it . . .

Ben Jonson's play, *Every Man out of his Humour* was acted in 1599, a few years after Shakespeare's arms were confirmed by the College of Heralds (See No. 9 in the list of documented facts). Some scholars believe that in this play Puntarvolo represents Francis Bacon because of the reference to his crest, which was a boar. (fig. 5) while Sogliardo represents the actor, Shakespeare, because of the pun on his motto, "Not Without Right", which has been changed in the play to "Not Without Mustard". We quote from Act iii Sc. 1:

*Sog.* Nay, I will have him, I am resolute for that, by this Parchment Gentlemen, I have ben so toil'd among the Harrots (Heralds) yonder, you will not beleeve, they doe speake i' the straungest language, and give a man the hardest terms for his money, that you ever knew.

| | |
|---|---|
| *Car.* | But ha' you arms, ha' you arms? |
| Sog. | Yfaith I thanke God I can write myself Gentleman now, Here's my Pattent, it cost me thirtie pounds by this breath. |
| *Punt.* | A very fair Coat, well Charg'd and full of Armorie. |
| *Sog.* | Nay it has as much varietie of colours in it, as you have seene a Coat have, how like you the Crest, Sir. |
| *Punt.* | I understand it not well, what is't? |
| *Sog.* | Marry Sir, it is your Bore without a head Rampant. |
| Punt. | A Bore without a head, that's very rare. |
| *Car.* | Aye, and rampant too: troth I commend the Herald's wit, he has deciphered him well: a Swine without a Head, without braine, wit, anything indeed, Ramping to Gentilitie. You can blazon the rest signior? can you not? |
| *Punt.* | Let the word (motto) be. Not without Mustard, your Crest is very rare, sir. |



## *A Brief Summary of the Life of Francis Bacon*

Philisopher, scientist, statesman and historian, Francis Bacon was one of the most remarkable men of the Elizabethan, or any other, era. Highly educated, well travelled and fluent in several languages, Bacon possessed all of the skills one would have expected to belong to the author of the Shakesperian works.

Born at York House, in the Strand, London on January 22, 1561, Francis was the son of Sir Nicholas Bacon and his second wife, Lady Anne. The elder Bacon, a leading English statesman during the reign of Queen Elizabeth, became Lord Keeper of the Great Seal of England and was one of the Queen's most influential advisors. Francis, youngest of the eight Bacon children, showed an early aptitude for learning and his father considered him to be the most likely of the children to follow his political career.

Lady Anne, sister-in-law to Lord Burghley, himself a leading advisor to the Queen, was one of the few highly educated women in England. The first lady-in-waiting to the Queen, Lady Anne was fluent in Greek and Latin and, with Sir Nicholas and tutors, she gave the young boy a solid educational foundation.

As a child, Francis was often in the presence of the Queen, who, marveling at his knowledge and quick wit, called him her "Little Lord Keeper." The Queen must have been looking to the future, to the time when Bacon would be an important member of the Court.

With that type of educational background, it was not considered unusual when Bacon entered Trinity College, Cambridge at the age of twelve. In that era, university training was based on ethics, natural philosophy, metaphysics and politics, primarily as expressed in the writings of the Greeks, notably Aristotle. Students proved their worth by defending theories, not by observing whether or not their beliefs were supported by fact. No effort was made to determine if this knowledge was practical. Barely a teenager, Bacon rebelled against this method arguing that it was "a philosophy only strong for disputations and contentions, but barren of the production of works for the benefit of man."

When he left the university in December 1575 at the age of fourteen, Bacon had already begun to form the ideas that were to be the basis of his life, from his public acts to his writing.

The first step towards a political career was the study of law and in June 1576, Bacon and his older brother, Anthony, entered Gray's Inn, one of London's leading law schools. Gray's Inn became an important part of his life. His classmates became lifelong friends, he participated in plays or revels and he maintained rooms there until his death.

Soon after entering the law school, however, Bacon's father arranged for him to accompany Sir Amyas Paulet, English Ambassador to France. The observant young man watched the intrigues of the French Court, saw how the mismanagement of the government was reflected in the lives of the people and had the opportunity to travel throughout the continent.

This great educational experience came to a sudden end in March 1579 with the death of his father. As the older brother, Anthony, inherited the estate and although he provided for his young brother, Francis was essentially on his own. He returned to Gray's Inn for more study and was admitted an outer barrister in 1582. Two years later, he was elected to the first of many terms as a member of Parliament.

An eloquent and outspoken legislator, Bacon continued to seek the favor of the Queen, hoping to rise in political influence. His political career stumbled, however, in 1593 when he opposed the Queen's intention to increase taxes. The Queen was deeply offended by the actions of her "Little Lord Keeper" and Bacon was banished from the court for a time. Although he became one of her advisors, his political advancement was curtailed until the Queen's death ten years later.

During this period, Bacon wrote his *Essays,* the *Colours of Good and Evil* and the *Meditations Sacrae,* and he began to form a relationship with the Earl of Essex, the Queen's favorite.

Bacon became advisor to the young ambitious Essex, though the latter rarely took anyone's advice. He did plead Bacon's case before the Queen and managed to get one minor position for him, but not the post Bacon desired. Essex's persistence on behalf of Bacon and his irrational actions, especially with the military, gave Bacon concern that he would be caught in the growing rift between the Queen and her favorite.

Bacon's worst fears were realized in 1601 when Essex devised a scheme to capture the Queen, force her to dismiss those he considered enemies and then to appoint himself as her advisor. The story is complicated but eventually, Essex was arrested and charged with treason. Bacon was ordered by the Queen to be one of the prosecutors against his friend. The Queen was not anxious to have Essex condemned but wanted to punish him for his actions. Bacon had warned his friend and patron that his highest loyalties remained with the Queen and in one instance, he reminded the court that it was straying from the issue at hand, treason. Essex was convicted and the Queen was reluctantly forced to have her favorite executed. Bacon was criticized for his role in the trial and in 1604, after the Queen's death, he issued his *Apology* in which he explained his actions. This document forms an important link to his authorship of the Shakespearian plays as noted in Chapter VI.

It was only after Elizabeth's death and the coronation of James I that Bacon's political fortunes began to improve. He was given knighthood in 1603 and soon after published his *Advancement of Learning,* dedicated to the King. In 1613, he was appointed attorney general, in 1618 Lord Chancellor and Baron Verulam and in 1621, Viscount St. Alban. In 1606, at age 45, he married fourteen year old Alice Barnham, daughter of a London alderman.

During this period, he wrote such works as *On the Wisdom of the Ancients: New Atlantis,* a Utopian fable; and the first part of *The Great Instauration,* or new beginning, called *Nova Organum.* In these books, and those which followed, Bacon set forth his plan for the future of mankind, a future where nature and man work in harmony. It was a bold and innovative philosophyand because of it, Bacon became famous throughout the intellectual centers of the world.

Bacon prepared for the 1621 session of Parliament with great anticipation. An internationally respected philosopher, he planned to use his position as Lord Chancellor to put forth his ideas for the betterment of man. Parliament had not been in session since 1614 and Bacon had great hopes that this Parliament would begin the process of reviewing laws and compiling them in a single book for the first time. Soon after Parliament opened, however, Bacon was charged with bribery and corruption in his activities as presiding officer of the Court of Chancery. One of the main duties of the Lord Chancellor was to conduct this court of equity or appeals. When Bacon assumed the position, there was a backlog of thousands of cases, but he drove himself tirelessly to eliminate the problem.

In those days, judges received no salaries and it was common for them to accept gifts and money from those appearing in court. Although Bacon was opposed to the system, he was a participant though quick to say he never allowed the money to sway his judgment. Often he ruled against those who provided what his enemies called bribes.

Without being given an opportunity to defend himself, Bacon was convicted of the charges. He was fined 40,000 pounds, sentenced to the Tower, prohibited from holding any office of the state, from sitting in Parliament or from coming within the verge (boundry) of the court. King James remitted the fine and released Bacon from the Tower in a few days with a pardon. Later he was allowed to approach the court, but his political career was over.

Bacon had been framed by his enemies but he retained his close friends, and although troubled with financial difficulties, his departure from public office allowed him to devote his remaining five years to writing. His *History of Henry VII* was published in 1622 and *Historia Ventorum* appeared the same year. In 1623, he completed *De Augmentis Scientarium,* a Latin translation with many additions to the *Advancement of Learning.* In these efforts he was often assisted by three men who were to become famous for their own work: playwright Ben Jonson, philosopher Thomas Hobbes and author George Herbert.

In his last years, Bacon hoped to produce a book of

scientific experiments. One day in late March 1626, he was travelling in the country and decided to investigate the effects of refrigeration by stuffing a chicken with snow. Bacon caught a chill and was carried to the near-by home of a friend. He died there on Easter Sunday, April 9, 1626.

Fig. 6 The Stratford monument, from Dugdale's *Warwickshire*.

## *Chapter II*
## *The Mystery of the Tombstone*

HAKSPERE died on April 23, 1616, and was buried in the Church of the Holy Trinity at Stratford-on-Avon. A monument containing his bust and bearing an inscription in stone was erected on the wall of the chancel by a person or persons unknown. This memorial must have been placed there between the time of Shakspere's death and the first mention of this monument by L. Digges in his poem in the 1623 First Folio, entitled *To the Memories of the deceased Author Maister VV. Shakespeare.* The fourth line contains these words, "thy Stratford Moniment", proving that the monument had been erected prior to 1623. The earliest illustration of it appears in Dugdale's *Antiquities of Warickshire,* published in 1656. In this illustration Shakspere is hugging a full sack against his body. There is no pen or paper. (fig. 6). Eight lines of writing are indicated but only the first two Latin words are given, "JUDICIO PYLIUM", the remaining lines being indicated by dots.

In the Rowe representation, found in his *Life of Shakespeare,* 1709, the artist may have found it too difficult to include the whole inscription, but he reproduces the entire Latin part (fig. 7).

*Judicio Pylium, Genio Socratem,*
*Arte Maronem,*
*Terra tegit, Populus maeret,*
*Olympus habet.*

(The judgment of Pylius, the genius of Socrates, the art of Virgil[1], he covers the world, the people admire him, Olympus has him).

In 1748, one hundred and thirty-two years after Shakespere's death, the original monument and bust were replaced by the one now seen in the church. The Reverend Kenrick, Vicar of the church, and Joseph Greene, Headmaster of the Stratford Grammar School reported that the original monument and bust through length of years and other accidents had become much impaired and decayed. John Ward, an actor who was in Stratford in 1746, conceived the idea of restoring it. He raised funds for this purpose by a performance of *Othello,* and work was commenced. He gave orders not only to repair but to beautify it, and the opportunity was taken to make a completely new representation of Shakspere (fig. 8). The new bust shows him holding a pen in his right hand and a paper under his left hand. The full sack has been replaced by a flat cushion with tassels. His head has been entirely changed. The face is full, with a mustache that turns up instead of down and a goatee in the style of 1748 replaces the drooping mustache and beard of the original bust. The inscription of eight lines, having been on stone, and placed on the wall, is probably the original engraving. It had two lines in Latin followed by six in English. The Latin has already been given. The English lines are as follows:

Fig. 7 Rowe's representation of the Stratford monument.

Stay Passenger, why goest thou by so fast?
Read if thou canst, whom envious death hath plast
with in this Monument Shakspeare: with whome
Quick nature dide: whose name doth deck $y^{s}$ Tombe.
Far more than cost: sieh all $y^{t}$ he hath writt.
leaves living art, but page, to serve his witt.
Obit ano. doi. 1616 AEtatis 53 DIE 23 Ap.

A stone was placed on the floor of the north side of the transept over Shakspere's grave. There is no record of the date when this stone was placed there or who put it there. No name appears on it; no date of birth or death.

George Steevens, (1736-1800), Shakespearian author and commentator, and Edmond Malone, (1741-1812), the Irish scholar and editor of *The Plays and Poems of William Shakespeare,* both stated that the inscription on the gravestone contained "an uncouth mixture of large and small letters". Each of these scholars published a reproduction of the inscription (figs. 9 and 41). Charles Knight (1791-1873), the English author and publisher, also visited the grave. He reproduced the epitaph in his *Biography of Shakspere,* showing an assortment of large and small letters that agreed with Stevens and Malone and he added the punctuation that they had omitted (fig. 10).

Knight comments, (p. 535): "It is very remarkable, we think, that this plain free-stone does not bear the name of Shakspere — has nothing to establish the fact that the stone originally belonged to his grave."

Because of the peculiar assortment of upper and lower case letters, as well as the words themselves, the original epitaph has been a curiosity and a puzzle to cryptographers and scholars for over one hundred and fifty years. They have sought without success to find a hidden message in it.

Fig. 8 The Stratford monument at the present time.

OF WILLIAM SHAKSPEARE. 129

Eſq; but, Mr. Granger juſtly obſerves, "as it is dated in 1610, before Janſen was in England, it is highly probable that it was not painted by him, at leaſt, that he did not paint it as a portrait of Shakſpeare."

Moſt of the other prints of Shakſpeare that have appeared, were copied from ſome or other of thoſe which I have mentioned. MALONE.

"The portrait palmed upon Mr. Pope" (I uſe the words of the late Mr. Oldys, in a Mſ. note to his copy of Langbaine,) "for an original of Shakſpeare, from which he had his fine plate engraven, is evidently a juvenile portrait of King James I." I am no judge in theſe matters, but only deliver an opinion, which if ill-grounded may be eaſily overthrown. The portrait to me at leaſt, has no traits of Shakſpeare.

STEEVENS.

4 *On his grave-ſtone underneath is, Good friend,* &c ] This epitaph is expreſſed in the following uncouth mixture of ſmall and capital letters:

Good Frend for Ieſus SAKE forbeare
To diGG TE Duſt EncloAſed HERe
Bleſe be TE Man $\overset{T}{Y}$ ſpares TEs Stones
And curſt be He $\overset{T}{Y}$ moves my Bones. STEEVENS.

5 *And curſt be he that moves my bones.*] It is uncertain whether this epitaph was written by Shakſpeare himſelf, or by one of his friends after his death. The imprecation contained in this laſt line, was perhaps ſuggeſted by an apprehenſion that our authour's remains might ſhare the ſame fate with thoſe of the reſt of his countrymen, and be added to the immenſe pile of human bones depoſited in the charnel-houſe at Stratford. This, however, is mere conjecture; for ſimilar execrations are found in many ancient Latin epitaphs.

Mr. Steevens has juſtly mentioned it as a ſingular circumſtance, that Shakſpeare does not appear to have written any verſes on his contemporaries, either in praiſe of the living, or in honour of the dead. I once imagined that he had mentioned Spenſer with kindneſs in one of his Sonnets; but have lately diſcovered that the ſonnet to which I allude, was written by Richard Barnefield. If, however, the following epitaphs be genuine, (and indeed the latter is much in Shakſpeare's manner,) he in two inſtances overcame that modeſt diffidence, which ſeems to have ſuppoſed the elogium of his humble muſe of no value.

In a Manuſcript volume of poems by William Herrick and others, in the hand-writing of the time of Charles I. which is among Rawlinſon's Collections in the Bodleian Library, is the following epitaph, aſcribed to our poet.

"AN EPITAPH.

"When God was pleas'd, the world unwilling yet,
"Elias James to nature payd his debt,
"And here reposeth; as he liv'd, he dyde;
"The ſaying in him ſtrongly verefide,—
"Such life, ſuch death: then, the known truth to tell,
"He liv'd a godly life, and dyde as well.

WM. SHAKSPEARE."

VOL. I. [I] There

Fig. 9 The tombstone inscription as copied by Steevens.

Good Frend for Iesus SAKE forbeare
To DiGG T-E Dust EncloAsed HE. Re.
Blese be T-E Man $\overset{T}{Y}$ spares T-Es Stones
And curst be He $\overset{T}{Y}$ moves my Bones.

There is a tradition that Shakspere (as Charles Knight spells the name in his *Biography)* was supposed to have written his own epitaph shortly before he died. There is the testimony of a gentleman, John Dowdall, who wrote from Warwickshire, 10 April 1693, to Edward Southwell:

> "Near the wall where his monument is erected lies the plain free-stone, underneath which his body is buried, with this epitaph made by himself a little before his death."[2]

He then quotes the epitaph and further states: "Not one for fear of the curse above saide, dare touch his gravestone, though his wife and daughters did earnestly desire to be laid in the same grave as himself."

There has been found in the Bodleian Library an old letter from a certain William Hall, a Queens College man, who took his B.A. degree in October 1694, to Edward Thwaites, of Queens College, a well-known Anglo-Saxon scholar. Halliwell-Phillips pronounced the letter genuine, and printed it for private circulation, with a preface, in which he showed that it was probably written in December 1694, seventy-eight years after Shakspere's death. Mr. Hall was visiting Stratford-on-Avon and wrote to his dear 'Neddy'. He quotes the famous lines on the tombstone, and added, "The little learning these verses contain would be a very strong argument of the want of it in the author." He said that Shakspere ordered these four lines to be cut on his tomb

## NOTE ON SOME POINTS OF SHAKSPERE'S WILL.

---

THE solemn clause, "My body to the earth whereof it is made," was carried into effect by the burial of William Shakspere in the chancel of his parish church. A tomb, of which we shall presently speak more particularly, was erected to his memory before 1623. The following lines are inscribed beneath the bust:—

"JVDICIO PYLIVM, GENIO SOCRATEM, ARTE MARONEM,
TERRA TEGIT, POPVLVS MÆRET, OLYMPVS HABET.

STAY PASSENGER, WHY GOEST THOV BY SO FAST,
READ, IF THOV CANST, WHOM ENVIOVS DEATH HATH PLAST
WITHIN THIS MONVMENT, SHAKSPEARE, WITH WHOME
QVICK NATVRE DIDE; WHOSE NAME DOTH DECK YS. TOMBE
FAR MORE THEN COST; SIEH ALL YT. HE HATH WRITT
LEAVES LIVING ART BVT PAGE TO SERVE HIS WITT.
OBIIT ANO. DOI. 1616. ÆTATIS 53. DIE 23. AP."

Below the monument, but at a few paces from the wall, is a flat stone, with the following extraordinary inscription:—

GOOD FREND FOR JESUS SAKE FORBEARE
TO DIGG T—E DUST ENCLOASED HE.RE.
BLESE BE T—E MAN $\overset{T}{Y}$ SPARES T—Es STONES
AND CURST BE HE $\overset{T}{Y}$ MOVES MY BONES.

In a letter from Warwickshire, in 1693,* the writer, after describing the monument to Shakspere, and giving its inscription, says, "Near the wall where this monument is erected lie the plain freestone underneath which his body is buried, with this epitaph made by himself a little before his death." He then gives the epitaph, and subsequently adds, "Not one for fear of the curse abovesaid dare touch his grave-stone, though his wife and daughters did earnestly desire to be laid in the same grave with him." This information is given by the tourist upon the authority of the clerk who showed him the church, who "was above eighty years old." Here is unquestionable authority for the existence of this free-stone seventy-seven years after the death of Shakspere. We have an earlier authority. In a plate to Dugdale's 'Antiquities of Warwickshire,' first published in 1656, we have a representation of Shakspere's tomb, with the following:—"Neare the wall where this monument is erected, lyeth a plain free-stone, underneath which his body is buried, with this epitaph—

Fig. 10 The tombstone inscription as copied by Knight.

stone during his lifetime, and that he did so because he feared that his bones might some day be removed; and he further said that "they buried him full seventeen feet deep — deep enough to secure him!"

There seems to be no reason to doubt the truth of the statement made by William Hall. He must have derived his information from common report in Stratford, as he was himself simply a traveler visiting the town.

Graves are not usually made deeper than six feet, as that is about the limit at which the grave digger can throw earth to the surface. To make a grave seventeen feet deep would require the same appliances used in digging a well, such as rope, windlass, buckets and so forth. This elaborate rigging and deep digging inside of the church would surely have been an unprecedented affair, one to have been talked about for several generations, certainly long enough for Mr. Hall to have heard it seventy-eight years later when he visited Stratford.

It is possible that a vault seventeen feet deep could have had a crypt for Shakespere's coffin and ample space as well to deposit the Shakespeare MMS which have never been found.

In Bacon's *Natural History,* (Century VIII, sec. 771) there is a passage that might be relevant to this remarkable tomb. He writes:

> "I remember Livy doth relate, that there were found at a time two coffins of lead in a tomb; whereof the one contained the body of King Numa, it being some four hundred years after his death; and the other, his books of sacred rites and ceremonies, and the discipline of the pontiffs; and that in the coffin that had the body, there was nothing to be seen, but a little light cinders around the sides; but in the coffin that had the books, they were found as fresh as if they had been newly written, being written on parchment, and covered over with watch-candles of wax, three or four fold."

The Diary of the Rev. John Ward, Vicar of Stratford in 1662, contains this interesting item:

"Shakespeare, Drayton and Ben Jonson had a merrie meeting and it seems drank too hard, for Shakespeare died of a feavor there contracted."

That epitaphs were discussed at these "merrie meetings" is revealed in a document preserved at Oxford University. This is the Ashmolean MS, which tells us that:

"Mr. Ben Jonson and Mr. William Shakespeare being merrie at a tavern, Mr. Jonson having begune this for his epitaph: 'Here lies Ben Jonson that was once one;' he gives it to Mr. Shakespeare to make up, who presently adds: 'Who while he lived was a sloe thing, and how being dead is nothinge'."

If we accept the evidence of the Ashmolean MS that epitaphs were discussed at these meetings, and also recall the tradition that Shakespere wrote his own epitaph before he died, is it too much to suggest that Ben Jonson might have had a hand in writing the inscription that appears on the tombstone? He might very well have added the curse at the end for two reasons: first, knowing that it would allay Shakspere's fear of having his bones removed, and second, to prevent the grave from being opened, thus preserving any documents hidden within the seventeen foot vault.

The carefully carved letters on the original tombstone were made in two distinct sizes which were not appropriate to the text (fig. 41). The biliteral cypher invented by Francis Bacon and illustrated by him in his *De Aug-*

*mentis Scientiarum* (The Advancement of Learning, 1623) is indicated.[3] But without the original stone to work from, the message cannot be deciphered, since the application of his cypher depends entirely upon the recognition of the slight differences that exist between the letters, both upper and lower case, of two almost identical alphabets. (fig. 11). Nevertheless, there *is* something concealed in the original text which anyone can find for himself.

The original tombstone was removed in 1831 and replaced by the one we now see. It will be noted that the original inscription was not carefully copied. In fact, it was so changed that any biliteral cypher it may have contained originally was destroyed.

It will always remain a mystery, an unanswerable question, whether someone had deciphered the message on the original tombstone inscription and had the stone removed and the inscription deliberately altered so that the message could not be read.

Neither the original nor the new tombstone contained the name of the person supposed to lie under it, or, as was the universal custom then as now, the date of birth and death.

For this information one must turn to the monument on the wall of the church, which gives his name, spelled 'Shakspeare', and the date of his death as 23 April 1616. It also mentions that he died in his 53rd year.

Finally there is the burial record of the Stratford-on-Avon Church of the Holy Trinity, which registers his name simply as "Will Shakspere, Gent."

Surprisingly the literary and theatrical worlds took no notice whatever of his death although it was the custom to honor the passing of their colleages by writing memorials at the time of their demise.

**Plate i.**

LIBER SEXTVS. 279

Exemplum *Alphabeti Biliterarij.*

| A | B | C | D | E | F |
|---|---|---|---|---|---|
| Aaaaa | aaaab | aaaba | aaabb | aabaa | aabab |
| G | H | I | K | L | M |
| aabba. | aabbb. | abaaa | abaab | ababa. | ababb |
| N | O | P | Q | R | S |
| abbaa. | abbab. | abbba. | abbbb. | baaaa. | baaab |
| T | V | W | X | Y | Z. |
| baaba. | baabb. | babaa. | babab. | babba. | babbb. |

Neque leue quiddam obitèr hoc modo perfectum est. Etenim ex hoc ipso patet Modus, quo ad omnem Loci Distantiam, per Obiecta, quæ vel Visui vel Auditui subijci possint, Sensa Animi proferre, & significare liceat, si modò Obiecta illa, duplicis tantum Differentiæ capacia sunt, veluti per Campanas, per Buccinas, per Flammeos, per Sonitus Tormentorum, & alia quæcunque. Verùm vt Inceptum persequamur, cùm ad Scribendum accingeris, Epistolam Interiorem in *Alphabetum* hoc *Biliterarium* solues. Sit Epistola interior;.

*Fuge.*

Exemplum *Solutionis.*

| F. | V. | G. | E. |
|---|---|---|---|
| Aabab. | baabb. | aabba. | aabaa. |

Præstò

Fig. 11 Bacon's biliteral cipher, *De Augmentis Scientiarum.*

London paid not the slightest attention to the passing of William Shakspere of Stratford-on-Avon. This is astonishing if he was considered to have been the author of the Shakespeare plays which had been frequently produced in London and at court by various companies for twenty-eight years.

This lack of tribute would seem to indicate that the literary world of London, in 1616, knew that "William Shakespeare" was not the Stratford actor but a pseudonym for a powerful person who wished to remain anonymous.

Fig. 12 Bacon's portrait, *Sylva Sylvarum*.

## *Chapter III*
## *The Magistrate, Mediocria Firma*

T is generally believed today that the controversy concerning the authorship of the Shakespeare works is quite recent, beginning in the middle of the nineteenth century. That this is not the case is supported by the fact that six prominent literary men of the Elizabethan period questioned the authorship of works attributed to William Shakespeare. These were:

1. Robert Greene (1558-1592), playwright and author of *A Groatsworth of Wit,* already alluded to in Documented Facts No. 6.

2. John Marston (1575-1634), English dramatist and satirist, whose father was a lecturer of the Middle Temple (Law School), London. Marston wrote *The Scourge of Villany* and *Pigmalion's Image* in 1598 under the pseudonym of W. Kinsayder and nine plays under his own name from 1600 to 1616. He received his B.A. degree from Oxford in 1592.

3. Joseph Hall (1574-1656), the earliest of the English satirists, who became Bishop of Exeter and later Bishop of Norwich.

4. William Covell (15  -1614), Cambridge graduate and

fellow of Queens College, 1589, and the author of *Polymanteia.*

5. Ben Jonson (1573-1637), Latin scholar, poet and playwright.

6. Thomas Nash (1567-1601), poet and playwright.

### *Greene, Marston, Hall*

Robert Greene, in *A Groatsworth of Wit,* as previously shown, had characterized "Shakescene" (the actor William Shakspere) as "an upstart crow beautified with our (author's) feathers . . ." He was followed by John Marston and Joseph Hall who published an exchange of witty and extremely revealing satires. We will first quote from Marston's *Reactio,* where, beginning on line 7, he reproaches the strict churchman, Joseph Hall, for his prudish attitude toward a poem that the literary censor had allowed to be published and had considered "exquisite". The poem under discussion was *Venus and Adonis,* which contained a letter of dedication to the Earl of Southampton, signed, in print, "William Shakespeare". Marston does not name the poem but refers to it as "those mirrors," because the story of the poem reflects Ovid's work, *Metamorphoses.* In his satire he questions Hall's intentions; is he going so far as to "wrack", (wreck) the "ancient honors" of the author, called the "Magistrate", and *Mediocria Firma?*

*Mediocria Firma* was the motto of the Bacon family. No other family in England could use it. (figs. 5 and 12). It appears on the Coat of Arms of Sir Nicholas Bacon, Francis Bacon's father, who had been the Lord Keeper of the Great Seal of England under Elizabeth, and was, of course, the motto used by his son, Francis, after his father's death. Sir Nicholas died in 1579 and Francis, then only 18, was recalled from the court of France, where he had been for two years.

By the time Marston's satire, *Reactio,* appeared in 1598, Francis Bacon had been a member of Parliament for 14 years, hence Marston's use of the term "Magistrate,"[1] coupled with the motto on the Bacon coat of Arms, *Mediocria Firma,* could only have pointed to Francis Bacon, as no other member of the Bacon family would have qualified.

The satire reads as follows:

REACTIO by John Marston
Page 62, beginning at line 7.

"Fie inconsiderate, it greeveth me
An Academick should so senceles be.
Fond Censurer! Why should those mirrors seeme
So vile to thee! Which better judgements deeme
Exquisite then, and in our polish'd times
May run for sencefull tollerable lines.
What, not mediocria firma from thy spight?
But must thy envious hungry fangs needs light
On Magistrates mirror? must thou needs detract
And strive to worke his antient honors wrack?"
(fig. 13)

The rare combination of words, 'honors wrack', which concludes this satire is also found in *Venus and Adonis* on line 558, and at this place there appears something not to be overlooked without closer scrutiny. The word 'backe' on line 557 appears, as if by design, to lie directly over the word 'honors'. Is this why Marston, the keen observer, lifts 'honors wrack,' out of *Venus and Adonis* just after using the Bacon family motto, *Mediocria firma?* Did he wish to call attention to this spot because he saw: that the first three letters of 'backe' joined with the 'o' and 'n' of honors directly below it made 'bacon'? (fig. 14).

62.

## REACTIO.

Is now ador'd: becaufe he furely knowes
Some-times it was defil'd with Popifh fhowes.
The Bells profane, and not to be endur'd,
Becaufe to Popifh rites they wereinur'd.
Pure madnes peace, ceafe to be infolent,
And be not outward fober, inlye impudent.
Fie inconfiderate, it greeueth me
An Academick fhould fo fenceles be.
Fond Cenfurer! Why fhould thofe mirrors feeme
So vile to thee? which better iudgements deeme
Exquifite then, and in our polifh'd times
May run for fencefull tollerable lines.
What, not *mediocria firma* from thy fpight?
But muft thy enuious hungry fangs needs light
On Magiftrates mirrour? muft thou needs detract
And ftriue to worke his antient honors wrack?

What

Fig. 13 *Reactio,* a satire by John Marston.

## VENVS AND ADONIS.

Now quicke defire hath caught the yeelding pray,
And gluttonlike fhe feeds, yet neuer filleth,
Her lips are conquerers, his lips obay,
Paying what ranfome the infulter willeth:
VVhofe vultur thought doth pitch the price fo hie,
That fhe will draw his lips rich treafure drie.

And hauing felt the fweetneffe of the fpoile,
VVith blind fold furie fhe begins to forrage,
Her face doth reeke,& fmoke,her blood doth boile,
And careleffe luft ftirs vp a defperat courage,
Planting obliuion, beating reafon backe,
Forgetting fhames pure blufh,& honors wracke.

Hot, faint, and wearie, with her hard imbracing,
Like a wild bird being tam'd with too much hãdling,
Or as the fleet-foot Roe that's tyr'd with chafing,
Or like the froward infant ftild with dandling:
He now obayes, and now no more refifteth,
VVhile fhe takes all fhe can, not all fhe lifteth.

VVhat waxe fo frozen but diffolues with tempring,
And yeelds at laft to euerie light impreffion?
Things out of hope, are compaft oft with ventring,
Chiefly in loue, whofe leaue exceeds commiffion:
Affection faints not like a pale-fac'd coward,
But thẽ woes beft, whẽ moft his choice is froward.

VVhen

ll. 547—570

Fig. 14 Lines 547-570, *Venus and Adonis.*

For fear of the literary censor, Marston would not have dared to have pointed out the close proximity of the five letters that spelled the name of the person he believed to be the true author of *Venus and Adonis*. He knew that the literary censor, Dr. Whitgift, had been the tutor of Francis Bacon at Cambridge. If Bacon wished to remain anonymous, Marston knew that Whitgift would have respected his wishes and would take action against anyone who revealed his *nom de plume*.

After the bold use of the Bacon motto, Marston and Hall seem to have decided to select an appropriate new name for Bacon as a substitute for *mediocria firma,* as this was too revealing a term for constant use. So they selected a person whose political life and occupation resembled Bacon's in many ways, a man who lived centuries before at the time of Ovid.

This man was the praetor, Marcus Antistius Labeo[2] whose undisguised and outspoken Republican sympathies had offended the Emperor Augustus, just as Francis Bacon, member of Parliament for Middlesex and Liverpool, had offended Queen Elizabeth by voting independently on a matter of taxation in 1593. Considering Bacon's belief in the divine right of kings he showed enormous courage in upholding the rights of the people by taking a stand against a measure proposed by the House of Lords which would have increased taxes. He knew that the Queen desired the passage of this measure, yet he voted against it and for his opposition Bacon was banished from Court for some time.

This caused quite a stir in London and of course Marston and Hall knew of it. Because they were Latin scholars they also knew the sequel to Labeo's opposition to the Emperor Augustus, which was that Capito, his political rival, was appointed to the consulate over his head by the Emperor. In a like manner Queen Elizabeth, on April 10, 1594, appointed Sir Edward Coke, Bacon's political rival, to be attorney-general in spite of the intercession on Bacon's behalf by the Queen's favorite, Essex. If the similarities in the political lives of these two men afforded Marston and Hall the opportunity to adopt the name Labeo to represent Bacon, there was still another and even more subtle similarity. Readers who are familiar with the widespread and frequent use of ciphers in Elizabethan correspondence will not be surprised to find that in selecting Marcus Antistius Labeo to stand for Bacon, rather than some other Roman jurist, they enjoyed doing so because "Labeo" has the same simple cipher count as Bacon, namely 33.

The Simple Cipher, based upon the 24-letter alphabet of the Elizabethan period, assigns numerical values to the letters: A=1, B=2, C=3, etc., but both I and J, being interchangeable, =9, and similarly, U and V =20. The Simple Cipher produces the number 33 for both names as follows:

| | | | |
|---|---|---|---|
| B= | 2 | L= | 11 |
| A= | 1 | A= | 1 |
| C= | 3 | B= | 2 |
| O= | 14 | E= | 5 |
| N= | 13 | O= | 14 |
| | 33 | | 33 |

The name Labeo was used in connection with two of the Shakespeare poems, *Venus and Adonis* and *The Rape of Lucrece*. Marston parodies two lines from the former poem which identifies it in his satire. He wrote, in his *Metamorphosis of Pigmalion's Image,* page 25, line 2:

"... So Labeo did complaine his love was stone,

25.

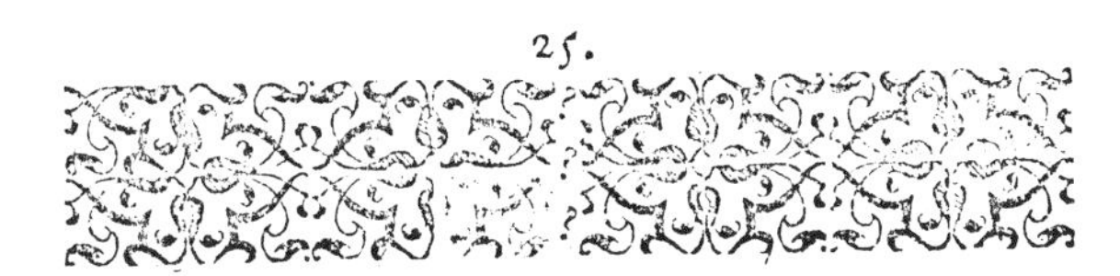

## of his Pigmalion.

*Pigmalion* hath a iolly boy begot.
So *Labeo* did complaine his loue was ſtone,
Obdurate, flinty, ſo relentleſſe none:
Yet *Lynceus* knowes; that in the end of this,
He wrought as ſtrange a metamorphoſis.
Ends not my Poem then ſurpaſſing ill?
Come, come, *Auguſtus*, crowne my laureat quill.
Now by the whyps of *Epigramatiſts*,
Ile not be laſht for my diſſembling ſhifts.
And therefore I vſe Popelings diſcipline,
Lay ope my faults to *Maſtigophoros* eyne:
Cenſure my ſelfe, fore others me deride.
And ſcoffe at mee, as if I had deni'd
Or thought my Poem good, when that I ſee
My lines are froth, my ſtanzaes ſapleſſe be.

C 2. Thus

Fig. 15 *Metamorphosis of Pigmalion's Image,* a satire by John Marston.

Obdurate, Flinty, so relentless none." (fig. 15)

The original, as it appears in the first quarto edition, 1593, of *Venus and Adonis,* 11. 199, reads:

"Art thou obdurate, flintie, hard as steele?
Nay more than flint, for stone at raine relenteth."

So it is not hard to see the connection between the two couplets and to conclude that Marston believed that Labeo, (Bacon) was the author of *Venus and Adonis.*

That it was the Shakespeare works that were being satirized is further proven by Marston's satire, *The Scourge of Villany,* in which the following lines include

Fig. 16 *The Scourage of Villany* by John Marston.

*Redde, age, quæ deinceps risisti.*

Whilst such huge Gyants shall affright our eyes
With execrable, damn'd impieties?
Shall I finde trading *Mecho*, neuer loath
Frankly to take a damning periur'd oath?
Shall *Furia* broke her sisters modesty,
And prostitute her soule to brothelry?
Shall *Cossus* make his well-fac'd wife a stale,
To yeeld his braided ware a quicker sale? stocks
Shall cock-horse, fat-paunch'd *Milo* staine whole
Of well borne soules, with his adultering spots?
Shall broking pandars sucke Nobility?
Soyling faire stems with foule impurity?
Nay, shall a trencher slaue extenuate,
Some *Lucrece* rape? and straight magnificate
Lewd *Iouian* lust? Whilst my satyrick vaine
Shall muzled be, not daring out to straine
His tearing paw? No gloomy *Iuvenall*,
Though to thy fortunes I disastrous fall.

*S A-*

both poems: (page 36, lines 15-19)

"Nay shall a trencher slave extenuate,
Some Lucrece rape? and straight magnificate
Lewd *Jovian* lust?[3] Whilst my satyrick vaine
Shall muzled be, not daring out to straine
His tearing paw? . . ."

Fig. 17 *Toothless Satire,* a satire by Joseph Hall.

26 LIB. II.

Might not (ſo they were pleaſd that beene aboue)
Long *Paper-abſtinence* our death remoue?
Then many a *Loller* would in forfaitment,
Beare *Paper-fagots* ore the Pauement.
But now men wager who ſhall blot the moſt,
And each man writes: *Ther's ſo much labour loſt.*
*That's good, that's great: Nay much is ſeldome well,*
*Of what is bad, a littl's a great deale.*
*Better is more: but beſt is nought at all.*
*Leſſe is the next, and leſſer criminall.*
*Little and good, is greateſt good ſaue one,*
*Then* Labeo, *or write little, or write none.*
Tuſh in ſmall paynes can be but little art,
Or lode full drie-fats fro the forren mart:
With *Folio-volumes,* two to an Oxe hide,
Or elſe ye *Pampheter* go ſtand aſide,
Read in each Schoole, in euery margent coted,
In euery Catalogue for an autour noted.
There's happineſſe well giuen, and well got,
Leſſe gifts, and leſſer gaines I weigh them not.
So

In the final lines Marston expresses his bitterness that his 'satyrick vaine' had been muzzled or 'stayed' i.e., put out of circulation by the censor. (Fig. 16)

Turning now to a satire by Joseph Hall it is found that in this one he connects Labeo with Shakespeare's *Love's Labour's Lost.* This play had been on the stage for some years previous to this satire, though not printed until 1598. Hall wrote, page 26, Lib. II, lines 6-12:

Ther's so much labour lost,
That's good, that's great: Nay much is seldome well,
Of what is bad, a littl's a great deal,
Better is more: but best is naught at all.
Lesse is the next, and lesser criminall.
Little and good, is greatest good save one,
Then *Labeo,* or write little, or write none. (fig. 17).

By shortening the first line and putting "labour lost" at the end of it, Hall calls attention to these words, which might otherwise be overlooked in the text. Here, in this position of emphasis they become a hint at the title of the play.

Let us now see what Joseph Hall has to say in his *Toothless Satire,* Lib. II, p. 25, Sat. I;

"For shame, write better *Labeo* or write none,
Or better write, or Labeo write alone.
Nay, call the Cynick but a wittie foole,
Thence to abjure his handsome drinking bole;
Because the thirsty swaine with hollow hand,
Convey'd the streame to weet his drie weasand.
*Write they that can, tho they that cannot do;*
*But who knows that, but they that do not know."*
(fig. 18)

The twenty-three year-old Joseph Hall was one of the first to find out that the Stratford actor could not write. He emphasized the point by printing the last two lines of his satire in italics, where he tells the reader very

FOr ſhame write better *Labeo*, or write none,
Or better write, or *Labeo* write alone.
Nay, call the *Cynick* but a wittie foole,
Thence to abiure his handſome drinking bole:
Becauſe the thirſtie ſwaine with hollow hand,
Conueyd the ſtreame to weet his drie weaſand.
*Write they that can, tho they that cannot do:*
*But who knowes that, but they that do not know.*
Lo what it is that makes white rags ſo deare,
That men muſt giue a teſton for a queare.
Lo what it is that makes gooſe-wings ſo ſcant,
That the diſtreſſed Semſter did them want.
So, lauiſh ope-tyde cauſeth faſting-lents,
And ſtaruling *Famine* comes of large expence.
Might

Fig. 18 *Toothless Satire,* a satire by Joseph Hall.

plainly that he and others are aware of this fact but pretend that they do not know it.

In the satire above there are several references of interest.

Line 3: "Nay, call the Cynick but a wittie foole,"
Here we have a word, cynick, that has lost one of its original meanings. In Elizabethan times a cynick could be defined as "one of a sect or school of philosophers founded by Antisthenes (444-365 B.C.) and of whom Diogenes was a disciple."[4] In this sense Francis Bacon would have qualified as a "Cynick".

Joseph Hall considered the "Cynick" to be a "wittie foole" to allow "the thirsty swaine" (the rustic actor) to take the credit for the Cynick's "handsome drinking bole", i.e., the Shakespeare works. Thus "the thirsty swaine" is allowed to quench his thirst in the Muses' stream while the real author, the Cynick-philosopher, Francis Bacon, remains hidden.

Lady Ann Bacon wrote, on 5 December 1594, to her two sons, Anthony and Francis, admonishing them "not to Mum nor Mask, nor sinfully Revel". She was worried about the prominent parts they were about to take in the *Gesta Grayorum,* or Grays Inn Revels. These Revels were to be given during the Christmas Holidays by the law students. According to his biographer, James Spedding, Francis Bacon wrote, among other things, the Councillor's Speeches for the *Knights of the Helmet.* This pageant-play was produced on 3 January 1595 as a part of the action.

The students pledged their allegiance symbolically to Pallas Athena, the Greek Goddess of Wisdom, Drama and the Fine Arts and the Protector of the State. The *Knights of the Helmet* swore to advance the ideals of Pallas Athena and after making their vows they kissed her Helmet, which conferred invisibility, and placed it on their heads. This ceremony caused a great stir and Hall refers to it in his *Byting Satires, Book IV, line 7, 1598.* This is one of the books of satires ordered "stayed", that is, taken out of circulation, by the literary censor, Whitgift, Archbishop of Canterbury.

*Labeo* is whip't, and laughs me in the face
Why? For I smite and hide the galled place,
Gird but the *Cynick's* Helmet on his head,
Cares he for Talus, or his flail of lead?
Long as the craftie *Cuttle* lieth sure
In the black Cloud of his thick vomiture;
Who list complaine of wronged faith or fame
When he may shift it on to another's name? (fig. 19)

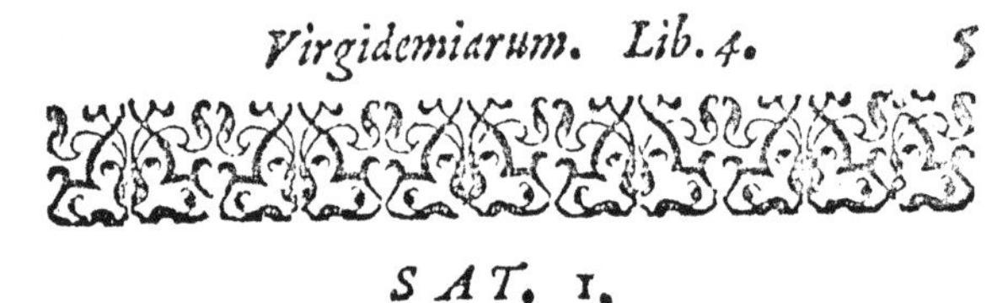
*Virgidemiarum. Lib. 4.* 5

SAT. I.

Bids all the Furies haunt ech peeuiſh line
That thus haue rackt their friendly readers eyne;
Worſe then the *Logogryphes* of later times,
Or *Hundreth Riddles* ſhak't to fleeue-leſſe rimes;
Should I endure theſe curſes and diſpight
While no mans eare ſhould glow at what I write?
*Labeo* is whip't, and laughs mee in the face
Why? for I ſmite and hide the galled-place,
Gird but the *Cynicks* Helmet on his head,
Cares hee for *Talus*, or his flayle of lead?
Long as the craftie *Cuttle* lieth ſure
In the blacke *Cloud* of his thicke vomiture;
Who liſt complaine of wronged faith or fame
When hee may ſhift it to anothers name?
*Caluus* can ſcratch his elbow, and can ſmile,
That thrift-leſſe *Pontice* bites his lip the while
Yet I intended in that ſelfe deuiſe,
To checke the churle for his knowne couetiſe.

B 3 Ech

Fig. 19 *Byting Satire* by John Marston.

The brilliant literary critic, Joseph Hall, who, as we have said, later became one of the prominent bishops of England, informs us in this satire that he has been whipping *Labeo,* that is, attacking him in print with his 'flail of lead' — the type; but *Labeo* only laughs. Why? Because *Labeo,* the *Cynick,* (Bacon) has only to place the Helmet of Pallas Athene on his head to become invisible behind his "black *Cloud*" of printer's ink. And if any one complains about the subject matter of the sex-poems, *Venus and Adonis* and *Lucrece* (his "thick vomiture"), he may shift the blame "on to another's name," William Shakespeare, his *nom de plume.*

Further use of the name Labeo may be found in still another satire by Hall:

> Tho' *Labeo* reaches right (who can deny?)
> The true strains of heroic poesy;
> For he can tell how fury reft his sense,
> And Phoebus filled him with intelligence.
> He can implore the heathen deities
> To guide his bold and busy enterprise;
> Or filch whole pages at a clap for need
> From honest Petrarch, clad in English weed:
> While big *but oh's!* each stanza can begin
> Whose trunk and tail sluttish and heartless been.
> He knows the grace of that new elegance,
> Which sweet Philsides fetch'd of late from France,
> That well beseem'd his high-styl'd Arcady
> Tho' others mar it with much liberty.
> In epithets to join two words in one,
> Forsooth, for adjectives can't stand alone;
> As a great poet could of Bacchus say,
> That he was *Semele-femori-gena.*
> Lastly he names the spirit of Astrophel.
> Now hath not *Labeo* done wondrous well?

The following are the Reverend Walter Begley's interpretations of this satire, beginning on p. 26 of Vol. II of his Bacon's *Nova Resuscetatio.*

"My commentary reads thus between the lines: 'Phoebus filled him'; Here we have the distich prefixed to *Venus and Adonis* brought into court again.

'mihi flavus *Apollo*
*Pocula* Castalia *plena ministret* aqua'

i.e., Phoebus Apollo would fill his cup.

'The heathen dieties (who) guide his bold and busy enterprise,' — Pallas Athena and Phoebus Apollo are meant.

'Or filch . . . from honest Petrarch,' — every one did this. Petrarch was the model of all courtly poets.

'While big *but oh's!* each stanza can begin,' — In *Lucrece* the very large proportion of thirty-two stanzas, each beginning with 'but' or 'oh' is found. There are fifteen stanzas beginning with 'but' and seventeen stanzas begin with 'oh', and in two cases more 'oh's' follow the first line.

'Philsides,' — This was Sir Philip Sidney, who was virtually the first to use compound English words, in his *Arcady* or *Arcadia*. He fetched this style from France and Bacon was the next man to adopt this *new elegance*.

'Others mar it,' — e.g., Nash and Harvey, who quite overdid the new style by barbarous exaggerations.

"In epithets to join two words in one,
Forsooth, for adjectives can't stand alone:"

As, for example, in *Lucrece,* line 384:

"And holie-thoughted Lucrece to their sight". And line 622:

"Thou backst reproch against long-living lawd." And lines 635 and 1782:

"This guilt would seem death-worthy in thy brother."

"Or keepe him from heart-casing words so long."

Actually the poems do not contain a great many compound words, but to the purist, Hall, it seemed that there were too many examples of this *new elegance*.

I give one more example of this *new elegance* of joining two words:

"And sometime where earth-delving conies keep."

W. S. Melsome, M.A., M.D., sometime fellow of Queens' College, Cambridge, who died in 1944 at Bath, has some interesting things to say about the example just quoted. In his *Bacon-Shakespeare Anatomy,* he writes:

"Bacon and Shakespeare were both interested in the 104th Psalm. Bacon in his verse translation writes of: "the digging conies" (Works, vii p. 282) while Shakespeare in the line 687 from *Venus and Adonis* quoted in the article in connection with the Cambridge expression, 'keeps', has "earth-delving Conies keep." But the Bible does not use either "digging" or "delving". Surely this helps to show that Bacon wrote *Venus and Adonis*. What the Bible says in the 104th Psalm is:

'The high hills are a refuge for the wild goats: and the rocks for the conies'.

In his *Apoththęgms,* Bacon tells a little joke about conies:

A company of scholars going together to catch conies, carried one scholar with them, which had not much more wit than he was born with; and to him they gave in charge that, if he saw any, he should be silent for fear of scaring them. But he no sooner espied a company of rabbits before the rest, but he cried aloud, "Ecce multi cuniculi!" which in English signifies, behold many conies; which he had no sooner said but the conies ran to their burrows; and he being checked by them for it answered "Who the devil would have thought that the rabbits understood Latin?"

As for the last of the quotation above, 'keep', Dr. Melsome writes several pages about the limited use of this word to signify 'living' or 'dwelling' and points out that it was, in Bacon's time, peculiar to Cambridge University. He writes:

"I had not been long at Cambridge before an undergraduate asked, 'Where do you keep?' As I hesitated to answer, he said, 'Do you live in college or in lodgings?' This word in this sense, is not used elsewhere in the British Empire. It occurs in Shakespeare in one tense or another (keep, keeps, keepest, kept).

1. "Knock at his study where they say he keeps." (Titus Andronicus, v. 2.5)
2. "A Spainard that keeps here in the court." (Love's Labour's Lost, iv. 1.99)
3. "As an outlaw in his castle keeps." (1 Henry 6, iii. 1.46)
4. "His chief followers lodge in towns . . . while he himself keeps in the corn field." (3 Henry 6, iv. 3.14)
5. "This habitation where thou keep'st." (ib., iii. 1.10)
6. "I will keep where there is wit stirring." (Trolius iii. 1.)
7. "Keeps still in Dunsinane." (Macbeth v. 4.9)

When Francis Bacon was entered at Trinity College, Cambridge in 1573, at the age of twelve, Philemon Holland was a minor fellow of the same college, and in 1601 his translation of Pliny's *Natural History* was published. In it is this passage: "where the pigmies by report do keep." Here is another example of a Cambridge man using 'keep' in the sense of 'living' or 'residing'. And although the word is now obsolete, it is, in this special sense, still used at Cambridge University.

### *William Covell*

Dr. Melsome continues:

"In 1595, two years after the publication of *Venus and Adonis,* William Covell, student of Christ's College, and afterwards fellow of Queens' College (1589) published in the University his *Polymanteia,* but did not put his name to it. There is a copy of it in the Cambridge University Library, another in the Bodleian at Oxford, another in the British Museum, and another in the Marsh Library in Dublin. There is also a copy of the second issue in the Folger Library at Washington with Covell's name to it, but I cannot hear of any copy of this second issue in the British Isles.

"This book tells us that the author of *Venus and Adonis* was educated in the University and afterwards at the Inns of Court; (the law schools of London) and you may guess which University by "where earth-delving conies keep," because the word "keep," in this sense, is not used in Oxford University nor was it used there in Bacon's time."

Dr. Melsome continues with a personal anecdote which is of interest:

"About twenty years ago an old Oxford scholar used to lunch with me and on one of these occasions there had been a leading article in *The Times* concerning the authorship of the Shakespeare plays. He had not seen it, but said the question had long ago been decided in Bacon's favour, and that in the sixties of the last century he and a few eminent Latin and Greek scholars in Oxford began to doubt whether a boy brought up in one of the grammar-schools which had recently been planted among the barbarians in England could have written *Hamlet* or *Love's Labour's Lost,* so they set to work investigating the true authorship, and their conclusion was unanimously in favour of Bacon. This was, I think, the first time that a group of men (scholars) had worked at the subject, although single individuals had already arrived at the same conclusion."[5]

Let us turn again to that indefatigable scholar, the Rev. Walter Begley, discoverer and editor of Milton's *Nova Solyma* and author of *Is it Shakespeare?, The Biblia Cabalistica* and *The Biblia Anagramatica* as well as Bacon's *Nova Resusitatio,* from which we now quote:

"If we read further (in these satires), we shall see that Hall knew a great deal about Francis Bacon's earlier work, and puts it in somewhat chronological order.

"There can hardly be more important new evidence than this, especially when we consider who gives it. Hall was one of the best literary critics of the time. He was well acquainted with members of the elder branch of the Bacon family, and afterwards travelled abroad with Edward Bacon, Francis Bacon's half-brother. Joseph Hall would therefore be a most likely man to know about the concealed work of Francis Bacon. In fact, if my interpretation should hold good, we have on excellent authority, in the few next lines, a summary of Bacon's literary work up to about 1596. This should be very important, for there is considerable 'concealment' about Bacon's early literary attempts, and many difficulties that need clearing up, and every little bit helps.

"Having suggested that *Labeo* 'hath done wondrous well', Hall proceeds to sketch his earlier attempts thus:

> But ere his Muse her weapon learn to wield,[6]
> Or dance a sober pirrhique in the field,
> Or marching wade in blood up to the knees,
> Her *arma virum* goes by two degrees.
> The sheep-cote first hath been her nursery,
> Where she hath worn her idle infancy,
> And in high startups[7] walk'd the pastur'd plains,
> To tend her tasked herd that there remains,
> And winded still a pipe of oat or beare;
> As did whilere the homely Carmelite,
> Following Virgil, and he Theocrite.

"In these important lines we have clearly allusions to *Titus Adronicus* marching through seas of blood, and to the contests of war of York and Lancaster, and other historical warlike plays of that period. We have also a fairly distinct allusion to "Lucrece" and to Bacon's magniloquent style generally.

"Hall tells us plainly enough that Bacon began with pastoral poetry. This may be lost, or may never have been published, I rather think, however, that Hall was referring to the 'Shepherds Kalendar' of 1579, and to Immerito's[8] share in it."

Unfortunately Hall and Marston had revealed too much in their satires and the works of these two champions of truth suffered a sad fate. Marston's satires were burned and Hall's were 'stayed' (taken out of circulation) by order of the literary censor, Dr. Whitgift, Archbishop of Canterbury, Francis Bacon's former tutor at Cambridge, and Dr. Barlow, Bishop of London.

Luckily for us a few copies escaped destruction; from these the facsimilies have been made.

### *Ben Jonson*

Now let us see what the fifth person, Ben Jonson, has to say about the authorship of *Venus and Adonis.* In his play, *The Poetaster,* published in 1602, the principal character is Ovid, a law student who spends his time writing poetry instead of studying the law. He has a servant, Luscus.

Act I, Scene 1

| | |
|---|---|
| Ovid. | *Then, when this bodie fals in funeral fire, my name shall live, and my best part aspire.* It shall go so. |
| Luscus. | Young master, Master Ovid, do you heare? Gods a me! away with your *songs* and *sonets:* and on with your gowne and Cappe, quickly: here, here, your Father will be a man of this roome presently. Come, nay, nay, nay, nay, be briefe. These verses too, a poyson on 'hem, I cannot abide 'hem, they make me redie to cast (vomit) by the bankes of *Helicon*[9]. Nay looke, what a rascally untoward thing this *Poetry* is; I could teare 'hem now. |
| Ovid. | Give mee, how neere's my Father? |
| Luscus. | Hart a'man; get a lawe booke in your hand, I will not answere you else. Why so: now there's some formalitie in you; By *Jove,* & three or foure of the Gods more, I am right of myne olde masters humour for that; this villanous *Poetry* will undoe you, by the Welkin. |
| Ovid. | What, hast thou buskins[10] on, *Luscus,* that thou swear'st so tragically and high? |
| Luscus. | No: but I have bootes on sir, and so ha's your father too by this time . . . Gods a mee! What'll you doe? why young master, you are not Castalian,[11] mad, lunatike, frantike, desperate? ha? |
| Ovid. | What ailest thou, *Luscus?* |
| Luscus. | God be with you sir, Ile leave you to your Poeticall fancies and *furies.* Ile not be guilty, I. *Exit.* |
| Ovid. | Be not, good ignorance: I'm glad th'art gone: for thus alone, our eare shall better judge the hastie errors of our morning *Muse* . . . *Kneele hindes to trash: me let bright Phoebus swell, With cups full flowing from the Muses Well.* |

These last two lines, which are in Jonson's italics, are his English translation of the two Latin lines that appear on the title page of *Venus and Adonis.*

*"Vilia miretur vulgus: mihi flavus Apollo*
*Pocula Castalia plena ministret aqua."*

These lines acknowledge the indebtedness of the author of *Venus and Adonis* to Ovid. Ben Jonson is therefore telling us that the author of the poem, *Venus and Adonis,* is a young law student who prefers writing poetry to studying the law. We know that this was true in Bacon's case from his own letters written early in his career; one of which contains the following lines: 17 November 1594: To my Lord of Essex:

"I am purposed not to follow the practice of the law, it drinketh too much time, which I have dedicated to better purpose."

Act I, Scene 1 of the *Poetaster* continues:

| | |
|---|---|
| Ovid. | *Then when this bodie fals in funerall fire, My name shall live, and my best part aspire.* |
| | *Enter Ovid Senior* |
| Ovid Sr. | Your name shall live indeede sir; you say true: but how infamously, how scorn'd and contemn'd in the eyes and eares of the best and gravest *Romanes,* that you think not on: you never so much as dreame of that. Are these the fruits of all my Travaile & Expenses? is this the Scope and Aime of thy studies? are these the hopeful courses wherwith I have so long flattered my expectation from thee? *Verses? Poetry? Ovid,* whom I thought to see the Pleader, become *Ovid* the Play-maker? |
| Ovid Jr. | No Sir. |

| | |
|---|---|
| Ovid Sr. | Yes Sir. I heare of a Tragedie of yours coming foorth for the common Players there, call'd *Medea*. By my housholde gods, if I come to the acting of it, I'le adde one tragicke part, more than is yet expected, to it: beleeve me when I promise it. What? shall I have my son a Stager now? an Enghle for Players? . . .Methinks if nothing else, yet this alone; the verie reading of the publike Edicts should fright thee from Commerce with them; and give thee distate enough of their actions. But this betrayes what a Student you are: this argues your proficiencie in the Law. |
| Ovid Jr. | They wrong me sir, and doe abuse you more, that blowe your eares with these untrue reports. I am not knowne unto the open Stage, nor doe I trafique in their *Theaters*. Indeede, I doe acknowledge, at request of some neare friends, and honorable Romaines I have begunne a Poeme of that nature. |
| Ovid Sr. | You have sir, a Poeme? and where is't? that's the Law you studie. |
| Ovid Jr. | *Cornelius Gallus* borrowed it to reade. |
| Ovid Sr. | *Cornelius Gallus?* Ther's another gallant, too, hath drunke of the same poyson: and *Tibullus* and *Propertius*. But these are Gentlemen of meanes, and Revenewes now. Thou art a younger brother, and hast nothing, but thy bare exhibition.[12] |

In the character of Ovid Senior, Ben Jonson accurately depicts for us the attitude of the upper classes and of the public edicts toward the theatre, actors and the writing of poetry and plays during the Elizabethan period. Ovid Senior says that he hears that his son has written a tragedy and threatens to create a tragedy of his own if it is put on the stage. Ovid Junior reassures his father that he is "not knowne unto the open Stage." He does not deny that he has been writing for the stage, only that he has not written openly.

Sir John Ferne, who was well known to the Bacons, studied law in the Inner Temple in 1586. He wrote *The Blazon of Gentrie* in which he tells how actors and playwrights are despised by gentlemen. One might write or act in a masque for the Court or his University, but to do so for money, for the vulgar spectators in a common theatre, was only worthy of dispraise and to be accounted infamous. The stage *stained* gentle blood.

Bacon was, of course, aware of this stigma and if he wrote for the stage, he would, like Ovid Junior, write anonymously or under a pseudonym. Furthermore, like Ovid Junior, he was a younger son and when his father Sir Nicholas died in 1579 young Francis was recalled from the court of France where he had been for two years. His elder brothers inherited the estates and Francis Bacon reluctantly began his law studies at Gray's Inn, as we know from his letters.

## *Thomas Nash*

Another poet and playwright of the period, Thomas Nash (1567-1601), in an address to the students of Cambridge, described the author of *Hamlet* in his Preface to Robert Greene's *Menaphon* in these words: "It is common practise nowadaies amongst a sort of shifting companions, that runne through every arte and thrive by none, to leave the trade of *Noverint* whereto they were born and busy themselves with the indevors of Art, that could scarcelie latinize their necke-verse if they should have neede: yet English *Seneca* read by candle light yeeldes manie good sentences, as Bloud is a begger, and so foorth; and if you intreate him faire in a frostie morn-

Students

*Cambridge*, it is no meruaile if euery alehouſe vaunt the table of the world turned vpſide down; ſince the childe beats his father, & the aſſe whippes his maſter. But leaſt I might ſeeme with theſe night crowes, *Nimis curioſus in aliena republica*. I'le turne backe to my firſt text, of ſtudies of delight; and talke a little in friendſhip with a few of our triuiall tranſlators. It is a cõmon practiſe now a daies amongſt a ſort of ſhifting companions, that runne through euery arte and thriue by none, to leaue the trade of *Nouerint* whereto they were borne, and buſie themſelues with the indeuors of Art, that could ſcarcelie latinize their necke-verſe if they ſhould haue neede; yet Engliſh *Seneca* read by candle light yeeldes manie good ſentences, as *Bloud is a begger*, and ſo foorth: and if you intreate him faire in a froſtie morning, he will affoord you whole *Hamlets*, I ſhould ſay handfulls of tragical ſpeaches. But ô griefe! *tempus edax rerum*, what's that will laſt alwaies? The ſea exhaled by droppes will in continuance be drie, and *Seneca* let bloud line by line and page by page, at length muſt needes die to our ſtage: which makes his famiſht followers to imitate the Kidde in *Æſop*, who enamored with the Foxes newfangles, forſooke all hopes of life to leape into a new occupation; and theſe men renowncing all poſsibilities of credit or eſtimation, to intermeddle with Italian tranſlations: wherein how poorelie they haue plodded, (as thoſe that are neither prouenzall men, nor are able to diſtinguiſh of Articles,) let all indifferent Gentlemen that haue trauailed in that tongue, diſcerne by their twopenie pamphlets: & no meruaile though their home-born mediocritie be ſuch in this matter; for what can be hoped of thoſe, that thruſt *Eliſium* into hell, and haue not learned ſo long as they haue liued in the ſpheares, the iuſt meaſure of the Horizon without an hexameter. Sufficeth them to bodge vp a blanke verſe with ifs and ands, & other while for recreation after their candle ſtuffe, hauing ſtarched their beardes moſt curiouſlie, to make a peripateticall path into the inner parts of the Citie, & ſpend two or three

** 3 howers

Fig. 20 A page from Nashe's Preface to Greene's *Menaphon*.

ing he will afford you whole Hamlets, I should say handfulls of tragical speaches." (fig. 20)

Francis Bacon was referred to as *Seneca* in 1594 in the *Attorney's Academy* by Thomas Powell, who calls him *"Good Seneca"*, and by Peter Boener in the preface to the Dutch edition of Bacon's *Essays*, Leyden, 1647, where Bacon is referred to as "a second *Seneca*".

Nash adds, further down, a sentence which reminds one of Marston's line, "what? not *mediocria firma* from thy spight." Nash writes: "These men renouncing all possibility of credit or estimation to intermeddle with Italian translations wherein how poorelie they have plodded (as those that are neither provenzall men, nor are able to distinguish of Articles) let all indifferent Gentlemen that travailed in that tongue, discerne by their two-penie pamphlets: & no mervaile though their *home-born mediocritie* be such in this matter." (My italics).

A man who "renounces all possibilities of credit or estimation" is obviously one who writes anonymously. An extraordinary number of the plays attributed to Shakespeare first appeared in quarto without an author's name on the title page. (See list of Plays that appeared in quarto p. 59).

The story of Hamlet was known to the Elizabethans in Francois de Belleforest's *Histoires tragiques,* (1559), and as early as 1588 or 1589, *Hamlet* had appeared on the English stage some years prior to its publication in quarto in 1603. This was the pirated first edition.

What was the trade of *Noverint* mentioned in Nash's *Preface?* "The trade of Noverint", to quote Lord Chief Justice John Campbell (1779-1861), a Shakespearian scholar, "is the profession of the Law, Jurisdiction, documents in former times always commencing with the words, 'Noverint universi per presentes', 'know all men by these presents'." Nash thus described the author of *Hamlet* as a lawyer and the son of a lawyer, "whereto he was born."

Thomas Nash is the sixth contemporary man of letters to describe the author of works attributed to Shakespeare as 'of the trade of noverint' — a lawyer. Hall and Marston described the author of *Venus and Adonis* as *Labeo,* a lawyer and magistrate at the time of Augustus and Ovid. Marston goes even further and refers to him as *"mediocria firma"* (Bacon) and as a "Magistrate". Ben Jonson describes the author of *Venus and Adonis* as a young law student who preferred writing poetry and tragedies to studying the law. William Covell considered the author of *Venus and Adonis* to be a graduate of Cambridge and of the Inner Temple — the law school.

Lord Cambell had this to say about the author of the plays and sonnets:

"He has a deep technical knowledge of the Law and an easy familiarity with some of the most abstruse proceedings in English Jurisprudence. One of the Sonnets, No. 46, is so intensely technical in its phraseology that without a considerable knowledge of English forensic procedure it cannot be fully understood. To Shakespeare's Law, lavishly as he propunds it, there can neither be demurrer, nor bill of exception, nor writ of error. The jests in the *Comedy of Errors* cannot be supposed to arise from anything in the laws of Syracuse, but they show the author to be very familiar with some of the most abstruse proceedings in English jurisprudence. Let a non-professional man, however astute, presume to talk law, and he will speedily fall into laughable absurdities."

Fig. 21 The interior of Gray's Inn hall.

Lord Campbell thus answers the Shakespearians who explain Shakespeare's knowledge of legal terms by stating that he picked them up in taverns or elsewhere!

The *Comedy of Errors* had its first performance on 28 December 1594 in the Great Hall of the Law School, Gray's Inn,[13] where Francis Bacon had his lodgings. (fig. 21) It was one of the events in a series of entertainments called the *Gesta Grayorum* (Gray's Inn Revels). It was during these Revels that the pagent-play of "The Honorable Order of the Knights of the Helmet" was given on 3 January 1595. The audience for these different events consisted of fellow lawyers and law students, statesmen and courtiers. Such an audience was unique in being able to appreciate the abstruse proceedings in English Jurisprudence which were referred to by Lord Campbell, who became, in 1850, Chief Justice of the Queen's Bench and later Lord Chancellor of England.

Fig. 22 The *Promus*, Folio 114, 27 January 1595.

## Chapter IV

## The Promus

contemporary manuscript known to contain phrases found in Shakespeare's plays is the *Promus of Formularies and Elagencies* of Francis Bacon. The Latin word, Promus, means store-room, or larder. This manuscript is in the British Museum, Harleian Collection, No. 7017. It was unknown to the public for more than two hundred years. The Promus contains 1655 phrases and expressions in English, Latin, Greek, French, Italian and Spanish. The entries are all in the handwriting of Francis Bacon, except for the French proverbs at the end. Permission was given by Mr. Maunde Thompson, keeper of MMS at the British Museum, to quote his authority in support of this assertion.

The earliest entry date is on Folio No. 85, 5 December 1594. The last entry date is on Folio No. 114, 27 January 1595. (fig. 22) The last Folio *number* is No. 132, but it is dateless.

Some of these phrases and expressions are used by Bacon in his prose works. Others appear verbatum, or only slightly changed, in the Shakespeare plays. The compiling of so many expressions and quotations in a large note book, and set down during such a short period of time, must have been done with a purpose in mind. Here are some examples:

| BACON'S PROMUS | SHAKESPEARE |
| --- | --- |
| To slay with a wooden sword.<br>Folio 98, No. 725, 1594-95. | Wounds like a wooden sword.<br>*Love's Labour's Lost.* v-2, Quarto 1598. |
| He that never clymb never fell.<br>Folio 92B, No. 484, 1594-95. | The art of the court, whose top<br>to climb is certain falling.<br>*Cymbeline,* iii-2, First Folio, 1623. |
| Mitte hanc de pectore curam.<br>Virgil, Aeneid. *Drive away this care from your mind.* Folio 86,<br>No. 182, 1594-95. | What sport shall we devise to drive<br>away the heavy thought of care?<br>Richard II, iii-4. Quarto 1597. |
| Haile of Perle.<br>Folio 101b, No. 872, 1594-95. | And hail rich pearles on thee.<br>*Anthony and Cleopatra,* ii-5,<br>First Folio 1623. |
| All is well that ends well.<br>Folio 103, No. 949, 1594-95. | *All's Well That Ends Well.*<br>First Folio 1623. |
| Hoc solum scio quod nihilscio.<br>*This only I know, that I know nothing.*<br>A saying of Socrates. Folio 87,<br>No. 191, 1594-95.<br><br>Also found in Bacon's *Novum Organum.*<br>"We know that we know nothing."<br><br>And again in his *De Augmentis,* 1622, he wrote,<br>"If you are wise you are a fool;<br>if you are a fool, you are wise. | A wise man knows himself to be a fool.<br>*As You Like It.* First Folio 1623. |
| Clavum clave pellere.<br>*One nail drives out another.*<br>Folio 101, No. 889, 1594-95. | One nail by strength drives out another.<br>*Two Gentlemen of Verona,* ii-4, First Folio 1623. |
| A fooles bolt is soone shott.<br>Folio 85, No. 106, 1594-95. | A fools bolt is soon shot.<br>*Henry V,* iii-7, First Folio 1623. |

| BACON'S PROMUS | SHAKESPEARE |
| --- | --- |
| Albada, (from a collection of Spanish salutations, "Good Dawning," (from the Spanish, alba, the dawn.) Folio 112, No. 1206, 1594-95. | Good Dawning[1] to thee friend, King Lear, ii-2, First Folio 1623. |
| Seldome cometh the better. Folio 92, No. 472, 1594-95. | Seldome cometh the better, I fear. Richard III, ii-3, Quarto 1597. |
| Good wine needs no bush.[2] Folio 93, No. 517, 1594-95. | Good wine needs no bush. *As You Like It,* Epilogue, First Folio 1623. |
| Galen's compositions not Paracelsus' separations. Folio 84, No. 85, 1594-95. | So I say both of Galen and Paracelsus. *All's Well That Ends Well.* ii-3, 1623. |
| In Folio 111, 1594-95, No. 1207 is "Golden sleepe", and entry No. 1215 is "Uprouse". These two are combined in *Romeo and Juliet.* | But where unbruished youth with unstuffed brain doth couch his limbs, there golden sleep doth reign. Therefore thy earliness doth me assure thou art uproused by some distemperature. Rom. Jul. ii-3, 1597. |
| Our sorrows are our school masters. (From the Greek). Folio 128, No. 1455, Undated. | Give sorrow leave awhile to tutor me. *Richard II,* iv-1. First Folio 1623. |
| | To wilful men, the injuries that they themselves procure, must be their schoolmasters. *King Lear,* ii-4. 1608, Quarto. |
| To fight with a shadow. Folio 99, No. 783, 1594-95. | He will fence with his own shadow. *Merchant of Venice,* x-2, 1600, Quarto. |
| Diluculo surgere salubrimum (sic). Folio 111, No. 1198, 1594-95. | *Diluculo surgere,* thou knowest. *Twelfth Night,* ii-3, First Folio 1623. |

| BACON'S PROMUS | SHAKESPEARE |
| --- | --- |
| To stumble at the threshold. Folio 99, No. 751, *(In limine offendere,* Erasamus. Ad. 184), 1594-95. | Many men that stumble at the threshold are well foretold that danger lurks within. *3 Henry VI,* iv-7, First Folio 1623. |
| En mangeant l'appetit vient. (Appetite comes by eating). Folio 131B, No. 1597, Undated. | As if increase of appetite had grown by what it feeds on. *Hamlet,* i-2, 1604 Quarto. Other women cloy the appetites they feed, but she makes hungry where most she satisfies. *Anthony and Cleopatra,* ii-3, First Folio 1623. |
| A thorn is gentle when it is young. Folio 93B, No. 537, 1594-96. | What! Can so young a thorn begin to prick. *3 Henry VI,* v-5, First Folio 1623. |
| Qui n'a patience n'a rien. (He who has not patience has nothing). Folio 131, No. 1566, Undated. | How poor are they that have not patience. *Othello,* ii-3, Quarto 1622. |
| Qui prete a l'ami perd au double. *(Who loans to a friend loses double).* Folio 130, No. 1468, Undated. | Loan oft loses both itself and friend. *Hamlet,* i-3. Quarto 1604. |
| Ex se finxit velut araneus. Erasamus, Ad. 918. *(He fabricated out of himself like a spider.* Folio 101, No. 797a. Undated. | My brain, more busy than the labouring spider, weaves tedious snares to trap mine enemies. *2 Henry VI,* iii-1, Quarto 1594. . . . but spider-like, out of his self-drawing web he gives us note . . . *Henry VIII,* i-1, First Folio 1623. |
| Conciliam homines mala. *A forein warre to appeas parties at home.* Folio 122, No. 1304, Undated. | Be it thy course to busy giddy minds with foreign quarrels. *2 Henry IV,* iv-5, Quarto 1600. |

BACON'S PROMUS

Nil tam bonum est quin male
narrando possit depravarier.
*(There is nothing so good that
it may not be perverted by reporting it ill).*
Folio 105B, No. 1072, 1594-95).

Optimum non nasci. Erasamus.
*('Tis best not to be born).*
Folio 104, No. 1004, 1594-95.

Ministerium meum honorificabo.
*(I will magnify mine office).*
Romans xi-13 (Vulgate).
Folio 86, No. 162, 1594-95.

There is no good accord where
every Jack would be a lord.
Folio 103b, No. 968, 1594-95.

Saying and doing are two things.
Folio 103b, 969, 1594-95.

SHAKESPEARE

Calumny the whitest virtue strikes.
*Measure for Measure.* ii-4. First Folio 1623.

Be thou as chaste as ice, as pure as snow,
thou shalt not escape calumny.
*Hamlet,* iii-1, Quarto 1604.

O welladay that ever I was born.
*Romeo & Julliet* iv-4. Quarto 1597.

Better my mother had not borne me.
*Hamlet* iii-1, Quarto 1604.

Clown: "Thou art not so long by
the head as honorificabilitudinitatibus."
*Love's Labour's Lost,* v-1, Quarto 1598.

Since every Jack became a gentleman,
there's many a gentle person made a Jack.
*Richard III,* i-3, 1597.

And ever may your highness yoke together
. . . my doing well with my well saying.
*Henry VIII,* iii-2, 1623.

Fear not my lord, we will not stand to prate; talkers are
no good
doers; be assured we came to use
our hands and not our tongues.
*Richard III,* i-3, 1597.

## 'S PROMUS

t losers have their words.
.. 103b, No. 972, 1594-95.

Better coming to the ending of a feast
than to the beginning of a fray.
Folio 103b, No. 977, 1594-95.

Suum cuique pulchrum. Eras. *(One's own is beautiful),*
Folio 103b, No. 981, 1594-95.

He had rather have his will than his wish.
Folio 85, No. 113, 1594-95.

The breath of flowers is sweetest in the air,
where it comes and goes like the warbling of music.
Essay of Gardens

## SHAKESPEARE

Then give me leave, for losers
will have leave to ease their
stomachs with their bitter tongues.
*Tit. Andr.* iii-1, 1594.

And well such losers may have leave to speak.
*2 Henry VI,* iii-1, 1594.

To the latter end of a fray and the
beginning of a feast, fits a dull
fighter and a keen guest.
*1 Henry IV,* iv-2, 1598.

An ill-favoured thing, sir, but mine own.
*As You Like It.,* v. 4, 1623.

So the maid that stood in the way for my wish
shall show me the way to my will.
*Henry V,* v-2, 1623.

That strain again! It had a dying fall,
O, it came o'er my ear like the sweet sound
That breathes upon a bank of violets
Stealing and giving odour.
The speech that opens Twelfth Night,
which was first performed in 1601-02,
but not published until the 1623 First Folio.

Many commentators, not being able to understand what can be meant by "sound" in relation to flowers, have altered it to "south". This comparison of musical sounds with the fragrance of flowers is so extraordinary that it is surely impossible that it should have occurred to two writers almost simultaneously.[3]

BACON

Some books are to be tasted: others to be swallowed;
and some few to be chewed and digested.
Essay of Studies

SHAKESPEARE

How shall we stretch our eye
When capital crimes, chew'd, swallow'd
and digested appear before us?
Henry V, II, ii.

---

In Folio 93, No. 516 of the Promus we also find this quotation from Erasamus (Ad. 725). Ljsdem e'literis efficitur tragaedia et comedia. *Tragedies and comedies are made of one alphabet.* This throws light upon the letter that Francis Bacon wrote to Sir Tobie Matthew in 1609:

> "I have sent you some copies of the *Advancement,* which you desired; and a little work of my recreation, which you desired not. My *Instauration* I reserve for our conference — it sleeps not. Those works of the *Alphabet* are in my opinion of less use to you where you are now, than at Paris."

J. Spedding, in his philosophical Works, 1.659 (1857), comments: "What these works of the 'alphabet' may have been I cannot guess; unless they relate to Bacon's cipher."

These are but a small number of the interesting instances of striking similarities between expressions found in Bacon's Promus and the Plays.

Equally arresting are those that exist between certain passages in Bacon's prose works and letters, and their close resemblances in the Shakespeare Plays. Here are some examples.

In a letter to Lord Rutland in 1596, Bacon wrote: "He that lives in fear doth die continually." In *Julius Caesar,* (1623), Act II Scene 2, we read: "Cowards die many times before their deaths."

Again in a letter to the same lord in 1596 Bacon wrote: "Like empty casks, they sound loud when a man knocks upon their outside." In *Henry V* (1623), Act III, Scene 4, we find: "The empty vessel makes the greatest sound."

In *Sylva Sylvarum* (1622-25), Bacon wrote: "Some who have kept chameleons a whole year together could never perceive that they fed upon anything but air." In *The Two Gentlemen of Verona* (1623), Act II, Scene 1, the same idea is expressed: "The chameleon, Love, can feed on the air."

Again from *Sylva Sylvarum,* Bacon wrote: "The people that dwell at the foot of snow mountains, by drinking snow water, have great bags hanging under their throats." In Shakespeare's *The Tempest,* Act 3, Scene 3, (1623), we read, "Who would believe that there were mountaineers, Dew-laptd like bulls, whose throats had hanging at 'em Wallets of flesh." Both of the observations refer, of course, to cases of goitre.

In his *Historia Densi et Rare* (1623), Bacon wrote: "Parchment is not only wrinkled in parts by fire but the whole body twists, curls and rolls up." And Shakespeare in *King John,* Act 5, Scene 7, writes: "I am a scribbled form, drawn with a pen upon a Parchment, and against this fire do I shrink up." Shakespeare, it should be remembered, died in 1616 and had been dead seven years before this play was printed in the 1623 First Folio.

Bacon, in *Sylva Sylvarum,* wrote: "Upon all poisons followeth swelling." In *Anthony and Cleopatra,* Act 5, Scene 2, (1623), we read: "If they had swallowed poison 'twould appear by external swelling."

Bacon in the *De Augmentis* used the expression: "These points and stings of words," and in Act 3, Scene 4 of Shakespeare's *All's Well That Ends Well* (1623), we find: "What sharp stings are in her mildest words."

In *The Charge against the Countess of Somerset* (1616), Bacon said, "He was of a thrasonical disposition," meaning bragging. The *American College Dictionary* defines this word as meaning boastful, vainglorious, and derived from the Latin *Thraso,* a boastful soldier in Terence's Eunuch. In *As You Like It* (1623), Act V, Scene 2, we find: " . . . and Caesars Thrasonicall bragge of I came, saw and overcome."

This unusual word also appears in *Love's Labor's Lost,* Act V, Scene 1, line 13, "his general behavior vaine, ridiculous and thrasonicall", Quarto 1598.

## Chapter V

## The Northumberland Manuscript

NLY one document written during the life of Francis Bacon and William Shakespeare has the names of both men on the same page. This is the Northumberland Manuscript, (fig. 23) found in Northumberland House, Strand, London, by John Bruce in 1867.

It was during the demolition of this mansion that an old black box was discovered containing various documents belonging to the Duke of Northumberland. Among the contents was a loose collection of sheets within a cover, now known as the Northumberland Manuscript. It showed signs of having been through a fire as the cover was burned at the edges.

The document was first edited by James Spedding with a facsimile of the cover only. In 1904, Mr. Frank Burgoyne, Librarian of the Lambeth Public Library, published a transcript with full facsimili of the contents, together with editorial notes. (fig. 24) He says: "The manuscript in its present condition contains forty-five leaves, so Mr. Spedding does not appear to have included the outside page (cover) in his enumeration. The pages are not numbered and there are no traces of stitching or sewing. It is therefore quite im-

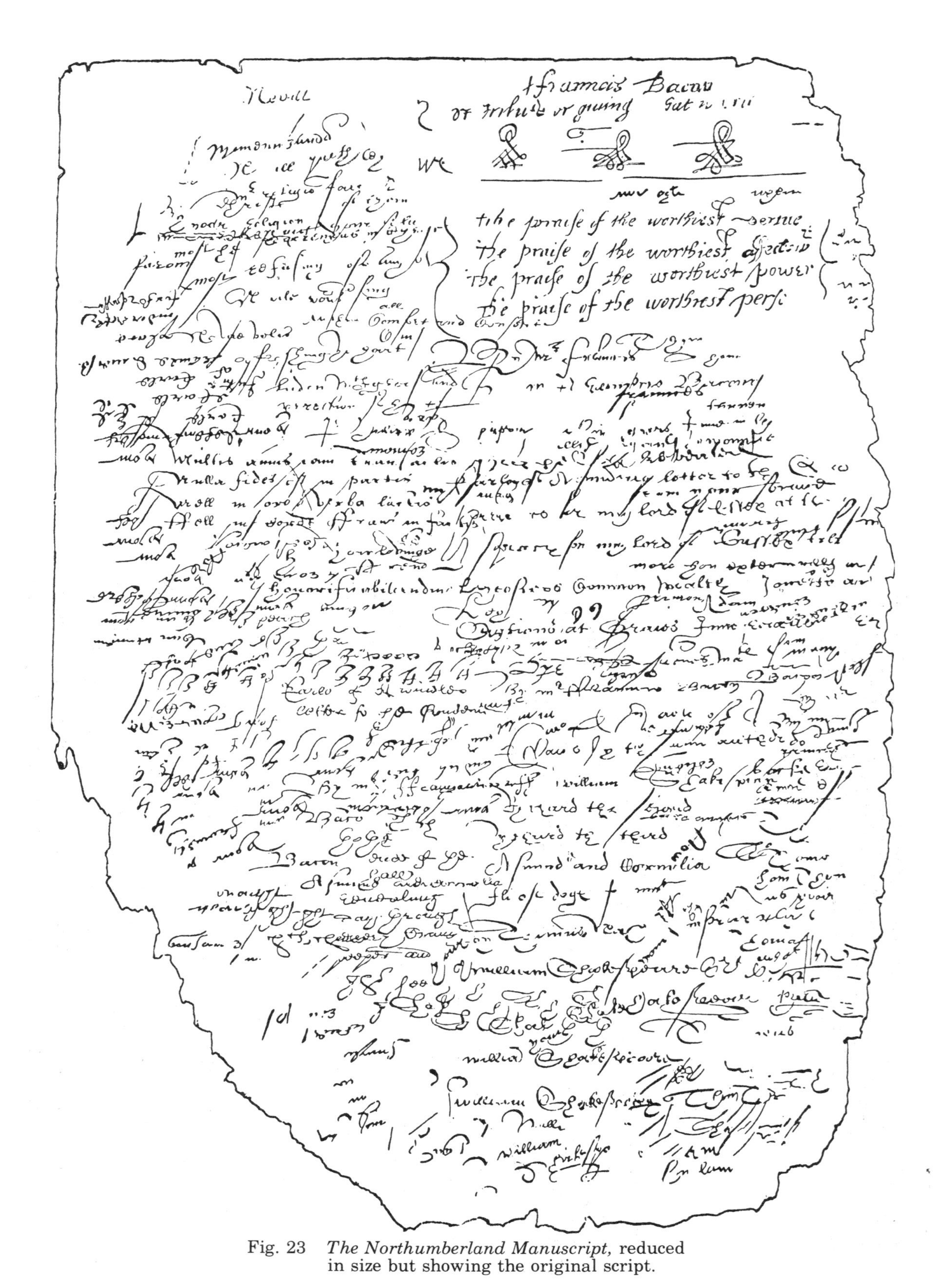

Francis Bacon

or tribute or giving

the praise of the worthiest vertue

the praise of the worthiest affection

the praise of the worthiest power

the praise of the worthiest persone

Fig. 23 *The Northumberland Manuscript,* reduced in size but showing the original script.

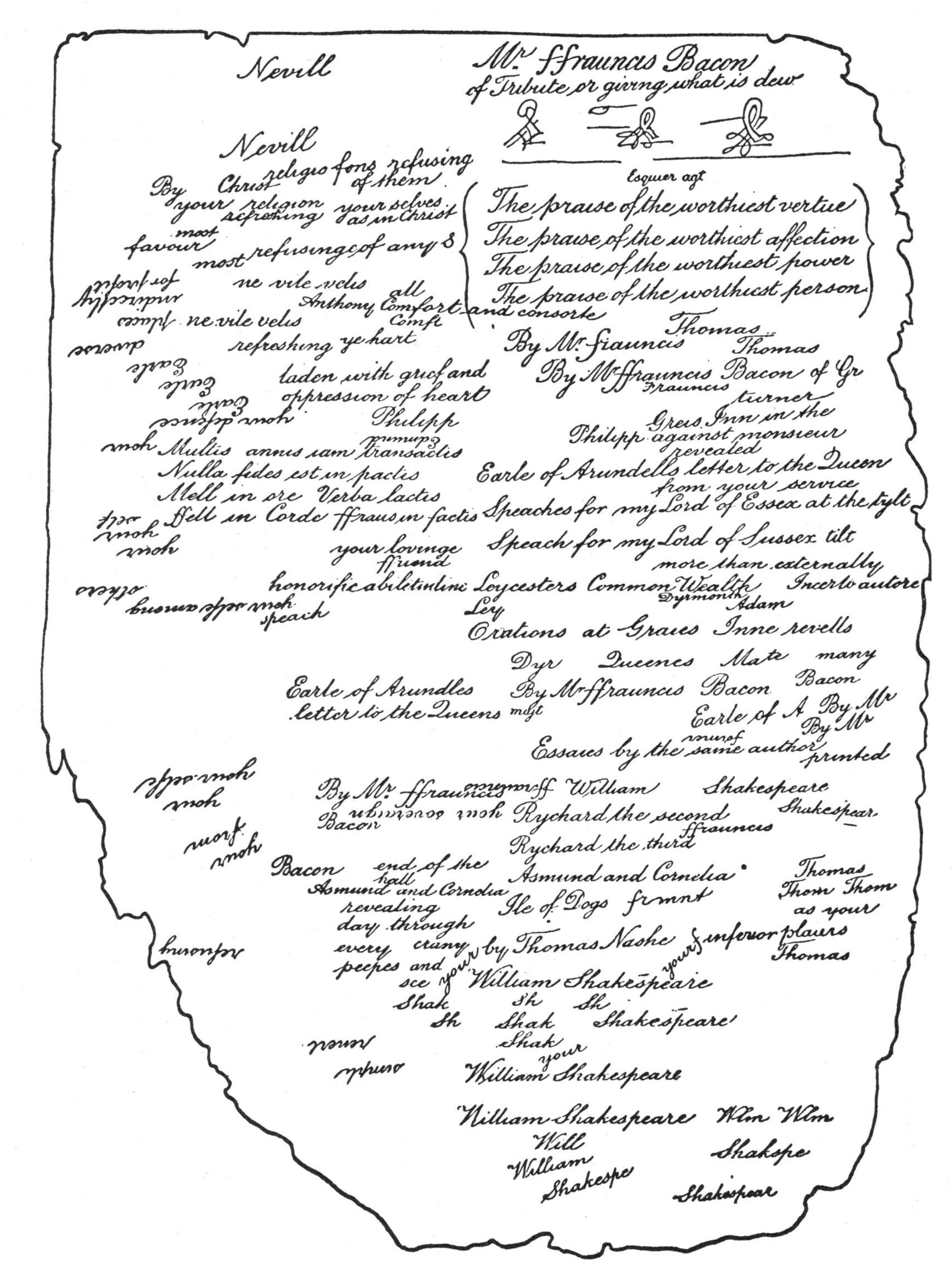


Fig. 24 The Northumberland Manuscript, reduced in size but showing the modern script.

possible even to conjecture what was the number of sheets in the original volume."

In another passage he says: "As to the penman who actually wrote the manuscript, nothing certain is known. The writing on the contents-page (cover) is chiefly in one hand, with occasional words in another, and a few words, mostly scrawled across the page at an angle, appear to be written by a third. The main body of the work is in two or more hand-writings . . . There are also notable breaks in folios 64 and 88, and the difference in penmanship in these pages is especially remarkable. This points to the collection having been written at a literary work-shop, or professional writers establishment. It is a fact worthy of notice that Bacon and his brother Anthony were interested in a business of the kind about the time suggested for the date of the writing of this book."

A photo facsimile of the cover of this manuscript, together with a reproduction in modern script are given so that the reader may obtain a better idea of it. About half way down on the right hand side may be seen some very interesting entries.

"Orations at Graies Inne Revells", then, "Dyr Queenes Mate -many-, Earle of Arundles letter to the Queens Majt . . . By Mr. ffrauncis Bacon . . . Earle of A . . . by Mr. . . ." and then, further down, "Essaies by the same author", and just below this, "printed". Then, nearer the middle we find, "By Mr. ffrauncis William Shakespeare" and directly under that is, "Rychard the second", "Rychard the third", with a "ffrauncis" in between the two titles of the plays. Richard II and Richard III are assumed to be the Shakespeare plays, since no other plays with those titles are known.

A little further down is written "Isle of Dogs frmnt (fragment?) by Thomas Nashe" and under that some trials in spelling Shakespeare, including two with a hyphen or dash over the middle 's'. This recalls the spelling on the title pages of the quartos of Hamlet and King Lear (figs. 49 and 46) and on the sonnets, "Shake-speare". We also find such variants as 'Shakspe, Shakespe, Shak, and Shakespear', the last without the final 'e'. There are also trials of William, such as 'Wlm and Will'.

A little to the left of the entry, "Isle of Dogs" are the words:

"Revealing day through every crany peepes".

In the *Rape of Lucrece,* lines 1086 and following we read:

> "Revealing day through every cranny spies,
> And seems to point her out where she sits weeping;
> To whom she sobbing speaks: 'O eye of eyes!
> Why pry'st thou through my window? leave thy peeping!"

In the printed poem 'peepes' becomes 'spies' to rime with 'eyes' and the last word of the next line ends with 'peeping'. As we compare these lines in the *Rape of Lucrece* with the writing that appears on the cover of the Northumberland Manuscript the connection is apparent.

On this same cover are found two additional entries that are of interest. The first is the word 'honorificabilitudini'. This peculiar word first appeared in print in a book called the *Catholicon,* published in France in 1460. It was used in the churches of France and in the Paris schools. As a young man Francis Bacon spent two years in France and travelled extensively on the Continent. He could have come across the book containing this word for he entered it in his Promus, in a shortened form, Folio 86; "Minesterium meum honorificabo". It appears in the long form in the first quarto edition 1598 of *Love's Labour's Lost* and in all subsequent editions as well, Act

V, scene 1, line 43;

Clown: "Thou art not so long by the head as honorificabilitudinitatibus."

The history of this peculiar word has been traced by Paget Toynbee, Writing in the Athenaeum, a London Weekly magazine, of 2 December 1899. He says that it is believed to have first appeared in the Latin Dictionary by Uguccione, called *Magnae Derivationes,* which was written before the invention of printing, in the latter half of the twelfth century and seems never to have been printed. Excerpts from it, however, were included in the Catholicon of Giovanni da Genova, one of the earliest of printed books that fall into the class known as 'incunabula', because they belong to the cradle of printing of the fifteenth century.

In this *Catholicon,* which, though undated, was printed before 1500, is found;

"Ab honorifico, hic et *hec honorificabilis, le* et *hec honorificabilituditatibus, – tis* et *hec honorificabilitudinitas,* et est longissima dictio, que illo versu continetur *Fulget Honorificabilitudinitatibus iste."*

Bacon realized that if he eliminated the prefix 'fulget' and the last word 'iste', he had an anagram which could be re-arranged to read:

HONORIFICABILITUDINITATIBUS

HI LUDI F. BACONIS NATI TUITI ORBI

or, translated from the Latin:

"These plays F. Bacon's offspring are preserved for the world."

Hi = these; Ludi = plays (as distinct from circus); Baconis = of Bacon; Nati = sons or offspring; Tuiti = passive passed participle of; tuti = saved or preserved; Orbi, dative singular of orbis = for the world.

It must have amused Bacon, who as his biographer says, could never pass by a jest, to put this long word into the mouth of the Clown in *Love's Labour's Lost.* For this play was the first Shakespeare play to be printed with an author's name on the title page of the first quarto: "By W. Shakespere, 1598". *Love's Labor's Lost* is not only the first instance where the author is named on the title page but it is also the only example of the name being spelled "Shakespere". All the other first quartos that are not anonymous spell the name "Shakespeare; Shak-speare: or Shake-speare.

The hyphenated form of the name, "Shake-speare", is identical with the hyphenated form of the name that may be seen in two places on the cover of the Northumberland Manuscript. Here, however, the hyphen is misplaced in the modern script and appears above the point of division of the name instead of between the two parts, as is clearly shown in the facsimile of the original writing.

That someone was experimenting with the name is shown in the Northumberland Manuscript in other places. A number of trial spellings may be seen as, for example, in addition to "William Shakespeare" some abbreviations, "Will", "Wlm" and "Shakspe" and even "Shak". This was Francis Bacon's own manuscript and, although the handwriting is not his, but is probably that of one of his "good pens," the appearance of these names and especially the one reading "By Mr. ffrauncis William Shakespeare" is not something to be referred to as mere "idle scribbling".

This manuscript must have belonged to Francis Bacon as we see from the heading at the top:

Mr. ffrauncis Bacon
of tribute or giving what is dew.

These two lines are separated from everything below by some symbols and a line. The heading shows that the cover once contained a number of Bacon's writings, such as the "Essaies by the same author", under which appears the word "printed". The two plays *'Rychard the second'* and *'Rychard the third'* must also have been included in the collection at one time as they are both listed on the cover.

The four lines in a bracket,

> The praise of the worthiest vertue
> The praise of the worthiest affection
> The praise of the worthiest power
> The praise of the worthiest person

are the titles and summary of Bacon's 'orations at Graies Inne revells', an entry to be seen at the top of the Northumberland Manuscript. Here is another indication that it had once belonged to Francis Bacon. In fact, many of the entries on the cover show that the collection contained letters written by Francis Bacon to Queen Elizabeth and letters he wrote for both Essex and the Earl of Arundle as well as speeches for 'My Lord of Sussex'.

The year Love Labor's Lost was published, 1598, was a crucial one for the hidden author of the Plays. The exchange of satires between Marston and Hall which had been going on for some time, had reached a point where the authorship of the plays was, by indirection, being attributed to Francis Bacon by the use of such names as *"Mediocria Firma", "The Magistrate"*, and *"Labeo"*.

All of these things must have alarmed the hidden author of the plays who had refrained from putting any name on the title page of the first seven quartos of the "anonymous" plays.

Something had to be done quickly to settle the matter of the authorship lest the career of the true author, if he had ambitions to rise in Court circles, be irreparably damaged because this would reveal his close association with the theatre. Three actions were taken: the burning and suppression of the satires upon the order of the literary censor, Dr. Whitgift, who had been Francis Bacon's tutor at Cambridge University, and the sudden appearance of a book, *Palladis Tamia, Wit's Treasury,* by Francis Meres, which flatly stated that all of the anonymous plays were by William Shakespeare. Meres must have known Bacon for he was the brother-in-law of John Florio, Bacon's tutor in Italian.

*Love's Labor's Lost* was the first of the Shakespeare plays to have an author's name printed on the title page and its publication and is the third event that took place during this crucial year. It gave Meres the opportunity to link the previous publications of plays that had been anonymous with this one and also to name them one by one so that there would be no misunderstanding.

Meres wrote: "As Plautis and Seneca are accounted the best among the Latines, so Shakespeare among ye English is the most excellent in both kinds for the stage: for Comedy witness his *Midsummers Night dreame* & his *Merchand of Venice,* for tragedy his *Richard 2, Richard 3, Henry the 4, King John, Titus Andronicus* and his *Romeo and Juliet;* for Comedy witness his *Getleme* (sic) *of Verona,* his *Errors,* his *Loves Labors lost,* his *Love Labours wonne*". So here we are told that eleven other plays are also Shakespeare's although only *Loues Labors lost,* at that time, 1598, bore his name on the title page.

*LIST OF THE PLAYS THAT APPEARED FOR THE FIRST TIME IN QUARTO EDITION*

| DATE OF 1st QUARTO | TITLE | AUTHOR | DATE OF 1st PERFORMANCE |
|---|---|---|---|
| 1594 | Titus Andronicus | Anonymous | 23 Jan. 1593-4*# |
| 1594 | 2 Henry VI | Anonymous | 3 Mar. 1591-2*# |
| 1595 | 3 Henry VI | Anonymous | 1589-92# |
| 1597 | Richard II | Anonymous | 1595-6# |
| 1597 | Richard III | Anonymous | 1592-3# |
| 1597 | Romeo and Juliet | Anonymous | 1594-5# |
| 1598 | Loves Labor's Lost | By W. Shakespere | 1594-5 |
| 1598 | 1 Henry IV | Anonymous | 1598-9 |
| 1600 | Henry V | Anonymous | 28 Nov. 1595* |
| 1600 | 2 Henry IV | Written by William Shakespeare | 1597-8 |
| 1600 | A Midsummer Night's Dream | Written by William Shakespeare | 1595-6 |
| 1600 | The Merchant of Venice | Written by William Shakespeare | 1596-7 |
| 1600 | Much Ado About Nothing | Written by William Shakespeare | 1598-9 |
| 1602 | The Merry Wives of Windsor | By William Shakespeare | 1600-01 |
| 1603 | Hamlet | By William Shake-speare | 11 June 1594* |
| 1608 | King Lear | M. William Shak-speare | 8 Apr. 1594* |
| 1609 | Troilus and Cressida | Written by William Shakespeare | 1601-02 |
| 1622 | Othello | Written by VVilliam Shakespeare | 1604-05 |

*Mentioned in Henslow's Diary
#Will refer to name of company playing this Play.

## ADDITIONAL PLAYS THAT APPEARED IN PRINT FOR THE FIRST TIME IN THE 1623 FIRST FOLIO

| NAME OF PLAY | DATE OF FIRST PERFORMANCE |
|---|---|
| The Tempest | 1611-12 |
| Two Gentlemen of Verona | 1594-95 |
| Measure for Measure | 1604-5 |
| The Comedy of Errors | 1592-93 |
| As You Like It | 1599-1600 |
| The Taming of the Shrew | 1593-94 |
| All is Well that Ends Well | 1602-03 |
| Twelfth Night, or What You Will | 1601-02 |
| The Winter's Tale | 1610-11 |
| The First Part of King Henry VI | 1589-92 |
| The Life of King Henry VIII | 1612-13 |
| Coriolanus | 1607-08 |
| Timon of Athens | 1607-08 |
| The Life and Death of Julius Ceasar | 1599-1600 |
| The Tragedy of Macbeth | 1605-06 |
| Cymbeline, King of Britaine | 1609-10 |
| King John | |

Fig. 25 Page from Bacon's *Apology*.

that book which was dedicated to my lord of Essex, being a story of the first year of king Henry IV. thinking it a seditious prelude to put into the people's head boldness and faction, said, She had an opinion that there was treason in it, and asked me if I could not find any places in it that might be drawn within case of treason: whereto I answered; For treason surely I found none, but for felony very many. And when her majesty hastily asked me, Wherein? I told her, the author had committed very apparent theft; for he had taken most of the sentences of Cornelius Tacitus, and translated them into English, and put them into his text. And another time when the queen would not be persuaded that it was his writing whose name was to it, but that it had some more mischievous author; and said with great indignation, That she would have him racked to produce his author: I replied; "Nay, madam, he is a doctor, never rack his person, but rack his style; let him have pen, ink, and paper, and help of books, and be enjoined to continue the story where it breaketh off, and I will undertake by collating the styles to judge whether he were the author or no." But for the main matter, sure I am, when the queen at any time asked mine opinion of my lord's case, I ever in one tenour said unto her; That they were faults which the law might term contempts;

## Chapter VI

## The Play of Richard II and Francis Bacon's part in the Trial of Essex.

HAKESPEARE'S only play that was mentioned at an Elizabethan or Jacobean state trial is Richard II. Both the play of Richard II and a book, or pamphlet, "The First Part of the Life and Raigne of King Henrie IV" written by John Hayward and dedicated to the Earl of Essex were mentioned during the Trial of Essex as having played a contributory part in the revolt.

Richard II was performed before an audience of nobles and other guests at Essex House, the home of Robert Devereux, the Earl of Essex, the evening before his disastrous rebellion. As mentioned at the trial, which took place in February, 1601, the play of Richard II was 'an old one'. It was first published anonymously in quarto in 1597, but it had been given in the theatres of London both before and after that date. However in those performances the scene in which Richard II was deposed had always been omitted because it could have given offense to Queen Elizabeth. But at the private performance at Essex House the deposition scene was included for the first time. It is clear that Essex used the deposition scene as a precedent to incite the nobles and other guests to support him in his uprising the following day. Although the play of Richard II was discussed at the trial the name of William Shakespeare was not even mentioned! Richard Burbage, the famous actor, who was the producer of Richard II, on this occasion, testified that "he had not wished to put on the play, since it was 'an old one', but, when paid 40s, he did so." In addition to the performance at Essex House, Queen Elizabeth stated "It had been played forty times in the open streets." The old Queen suspected that these performances were given with a purpose and she is known to have said angrily, "Know ye not that I am Richard II"?

The seditious book, or pamphlet, written by Dr. Hayward, who was committed to the Tower for it, had much incensed Queen Elizabeth. She asked Bacon, being then her Councel Learned, whether there were any treason in it. Bacon, intending to do him, (Dr. Hayward) a pleasure, and take off the Queen's bitterness with a merry conceit, answered; "No Madam, for treason I cannot deliver an opinion that there is any, but very much Felony." The Queen asked, "How? Wherein?" Bacon answered, "Because he hath stolen many of his sentences and conceits out of Cornelius Tacitus, and translated them into English and put them into his text." This fact has only recently been discovered by Shakespearian scholars:

Bacon wrote, in his Apology', p. 218; (fig. 25) "Another time, when the queen would not be persuaded that it was his writing whose name was to it but that it had some more mischievous author, and said with great indignation, that she would have him racked to produce his author, I replied 'Nay madam, he is a doctor, never rack his person but rack his style; let him have pen and paper and help of books, and be enjoyned to continue the story where it breaketh off, and I will undertake, by collecting the styles to judge whether he were the author or no.' "



Fig. 26 Page from Bacon's *Apology*.

after, whereby to do my lord service. Hereupon the next news that I heard was, that we were all sent for again; and that her majesty's pleasure was, we all should have parts in the business; and the lords falling into distribution of our parts, it was allotted to me, that I should set forth some undutiful carriage of my lord, in giving occasion and countenance to a seditious pamphlet, as it was termed, which was dedicated unto him, which was the book before mentioned of king Henry IV. Whereupon I replied to that allotment, and said to their lordships, That it was an old matter, and had no manner of coherence with the rest of the charge, being matters of Ireland: and therefore, that I having been wronged by bruits before, this would expose me to them more; and it would be said I gave in evidence mine own tales. It was answered again

Bacon continues in his Apology, p. 218

"About the same time I remember an answer of mine in a matter that had some affinity with my lord's cause, which though it grew from me went after about in other's names." In other words he admits that he used a nom-de-plume.

And on p. 222 (fig. 26): Bacon says;

"I having been wronged by bruits (rumours) before, this would expose me to them more; and it would be said I gave in evidence mine own tales."

In these statements Bacon admits for the first and only time in his life several things of great importance: 1) That he was the author of writings that went about in other's names. 2) that these writings were connected with the Trial of Essex and that Bacon, as the queen's Councel Learned could not give them in evidence because it would be said that he gave in evidence his own tales. Therefore he must have written the play of Richard II as this was the only play under discussion at the trial.

Fig. 27 *The First Part of Youth's Errors* by Thomas Bushel.

THE

FIRST

PART

OF

*Youths Errors.*

*Written by* THOMAS BVSHEL, *the Superlatiue Prodigall.*

Luke 15. 18.

*I will ariſe and goe to my Father, and ſay vnto him, Father, I haue ſinned againſt heauen and before thee, and am no more worthy to be called thy ſonne, &c.*

Imprinted at London. 1628.

126

*To his approued beloued Mr.* Iohn Eliot *Eſquire.*

He ample teſtimony of your true affection to wards my Lord *Verulam* Viſcount Saint *Albans*, hath obliged me your ſeruant. Yet leaſt the calumnious tongues of men might extenuate the good opinion you had of his worth and merit: I muſt ingenuouſly confeſſe that my ſelfe and others of his ſeruants were the occaſion of exhaling his vertues into

127

into a darke eclipſe; which God knowes would haue long endur'd both for the honour of his King, and good of the commonaltie; had not we whom his bounty nurſed, laid on his guiltleſſe ſhoulders our baſe and execrable deeds to be ſcand and cenſur'de by the whole Senate of a ſtate, where no ſooner ſentence was giuen, but moſt of vs forſooke him, which makes vs beare the badge of Iewes to this day. Yet I am confident, there were ſome Godly Daniels amongſt vs; howſoeuer I will not mention any for feare of attributing more then their due, and offending others; but leaue the ſequel to their owne conſciences, who can beſt iudge of innocencie. As for

128

for my ſelfe with ſhame I muſt acquite the title, and pleade guilty; which grieues my very ſoule, that ſo matchleſſe a Peere ſhould bee loſt by ſuch inſinuating caterpillars, who in his owne nature ſcorn'de the leaſt thought of any baſe, vnworthy, or ignoble act, though ſubiect to infirmities, as ordain'de to the wiſeſt: for ſo much I muſt aſſure you was his hatred to bribery, corruption, or ſymmonie, that hearing I had receiu'de the profits of firſt fruits for a Beneficе, which his pious charitie freely gaue, preſently ſent to me, and being asked of his Lordſhip, I ſodainly confeſſed, whereupon hee fell into ſo great a paſſion, that repli'de, I was curſed in my

## *Chapter VII*
## *Contemporary Evidence Supporting Bacon*

HILE searching for contemporary evidence about Bacon there were found many testimonials of his character which were so different from the opinions of him held by the majority of uninformed persons today, that it was thought necessary to make a more intensive search in order to find out how this misunderstanding arose. The principal offender seems to have been Thomas Babington Macaulay, who, in his essay on Bacon, written more than two hundred years after Bacon's death in 1626, laid the foundation for the present misunderstanding.

The result is that from 1837 to the present time many English speaking people have thought with Macaulay that Bacon basely received bribes when in a high official position and treated Essex and sundry persons in ways that were abominable, ungrateful and unjustifiable. To accept Macaulay's charges against Bacon as having been proven is unjustifiable. For example, the Rt. Honorable Winston L.S. Churchill has this to say about Macaulay in *Marlborough, His Life and Times:* "Macaulay with his captivating style and devastating self-confidence was the prince of literary rogues who always preferred the tale to the truth and smirched or glorified great men according as they affected his drama." So true is this estimate that the University of Oxford has ordered all of Macaulay's works to be placed in a special category as "not trustworthy for History."

In 1882 J. Cotter Morison wrote a book on Lord Macaulay which was reprinted in 1908 in the *English Men of Letters* series, published by Macmillan & Co.

"We now come, not without reluctance, to look at the deplorable article on Bacon.

"The historical portion has only just lately received such an exposure at the hands of the late J. Spedding (the biographer of Francis Bacon), that to dwell upon it here is as unnecessary as it would be impertinent. Two octavo volumes were not found more than sufficient to set forth the full proofs of Macaulay's quite astounding inaccuracies, misrepresentations, and even falsifications of truth."

Spedding in his biography of Francis Bacon and in his *Evenings with a Reviewer* has fully exonerated Bacon of any disloyalty to Essex. Basil Montagu, in his *Life of Bacon,* has also been attacked by Macaulay in his Essay on Bacon.

As for the charges that have been made against Bacon that he was a corrupt judge and took bribes we have testimony to the contrary from several sources. Bacon himself said; 'I am not guilty of any unworthyness except perhaps too much softness in the beginning of my troubles.

This 'softness' seems to have consisted of allowing his trusted servants too much liberty. One of these, Thomas Bushel, gives this testimony to his master's character in his book, *The First Part of Youth's Errors,* a rare and little known volume that is of the greatest importance in clearing Bacon of the unjust charges of accepting bribes and of being a corrupt judge, charges that are repeated by those who take not the slightest interest in discovering whether or not they were well founded. Speaking of my Lord Verulam, Bushel writes: (fig. 27)

> "I must ingenously confess that myselfe and others of his servants were the occasion of exhaling his vertues into a dark eclipse; which God knows would have long endured both for the honour of his King, and the good of the Commonalite; had not we whom his bountie nursed, laid on his guiltless shoulders our base and exerable deeds to be scand and censured by the whole Senate of a state, where no sooner sentence was given, but most of us forsook him .... Yet I am confident that there were some Godly Daniels among us .... As for myself with shame I must acquit the title and pleade guilty; which grieves my very soule, that so matchless a Peer should be lost by such insinuating caterpillers, who in his owne nature scorn'd the least thought of any base, unworthy, or ignoble act, though subject to infirmities, as ordain'de to the wisest; for so much I must assure you was his hatred to bribery, corruption, or symmonie, that hearing that I had reciv'de the profits of first fruits for a Benefice, which his pious charitie freely gave, presently sent to me, and being asked of his Lordship, I sodainly confessed, whereupon he fell into so great a passion that (he) replied that I was cursed ...................."

For their own protection the Elizabethans had to be masters of the art of concealment and of making veiled allusions. Anagrams were as popular in that period as cross word puzzles are today. In view of what follows, the derivation of the word *anagram* is significant. The word comes from the two Greek words *ana,* back, again, and *gramma,* to write. It originally meant the letters of a word spelled backwards, but in its usual wider sense the change of one word or phrase into another by the transposition of the letters.

For example the English historian, William Camden, (1551-1623), wrote all of his works in Latin and he secreted his name in his *Remains concerning Britain* in the Latin phrases found on the title page. One of them is DUM ILLA EVINCAM and the other is NIL MALUM CUI DEA. In the Elizabethan alphabet of twenty four letters U and V, like I and J, were interchangeable. In the first Latin example the *u* of *dum* and the *V* of *EVINCAM* make the *W* of *William* and in the second the two *Us* make the *W*. So in both examples the name *William Camden* is revealed as the author of the book.

D'Israeli said, "Anagrams were in the Elizabethan and Jacobean times, the fashionable amusement of the wittest and most learned."

Galileo Galilei (1564-1642) used an anagram to protect his discovery that Venus had phases like the moon. This protected his claim until he was ready to announce it to the world![1]

Francis Bacon would certainly have been aware of this clever form of concealment and he probably used the extraordinary word "honorificabilitudinitatibus" in *Loves Labours Lost* for the same reason, to protect for posterity his authorship of this play.

In the *American Conservator,* in 1905, a Dr. Platt gave an ingenious solution of the riddle in *Loves Labours Lost:*

> Moth. What is AB spelt backwards with a horn on his head?
>
> Holofernes. BA, *pueritia,*[2] with a horn added.

Dr. Platt claims to have discovered that a horn-shaped mark at the beginning of a word-on the head- in Elizabethan legal documents and printing was used for the legal term CON. If Bacon had written the play and asked this curious riddle containing the first two letters of his name, we should expect to find it capable of providing the second syllable of his surname. The dialogue is a discussion or quibble about the "horn book", or ABC. The next letter to AB is, of course, C; and "spelt backward" it is BAC. Denham Parsons has recently pointed out that "C" is the letter anciently associated with the horns of a crescent moon, and refers to Lindsay's *Notae Latinae,* pp. XIII., 28-34, 333, on the use of the C *conversum* as a symbol of English lawyers for "Con". Then, "AB with a horn on his head" is **Ↄ** AB, and backward it is BA**Ↄ** or BACON. An official of the Public Records Office said that **Ↄ** was a common abbreviation for "CON". This is confirmed by *The Record Interpreter* by C.T. Martin, (London 1892). It is also mentioned and illustrated in a dictionary of abbreviations, called *Lexicon Diplomaticon,* published in 1756.

*Loves Labours Lost* was the first of the Shakespeare plays which gave the name of the author on the title page of the first quarto: "By W. Shakespere". The spelling in this one instance lacks the 'a' in the second syllable of Shakespeare. It is as though Bacon had not quite decided upon the spelling of his nom-de-plume, this being the first time that an author's name was given. The early Shakespearian plays gave no author's name on the title page of their respective first quartos, as previously shown in Chapter V.

Bacon had a good reason for writing anonymously. He had the example of what happened to his father, Sir Nicholas Bacon, who had put his name to a work that had offended Queen Elizabeth with the result that there was a stay in his fortunes and he was prevented from becoming a Privy Councellor. At a later date, in order not to take the chance of offending the Queen again, it is said he published his writings under the name of a living man. This method of concealed authorship was so successful that he eventually rose to become the Lord Keeper of the Seal, while his second wife, Lady Ann Bacon, became Head Lady in Waiting to the Queen.

It is hardly surprising therefore, to find that their son Francis Bacon, when writing for the theater, adopted a similar method of concealment by first writing anonymously and then using as a pseudonym the name of a living person, the actor William Shakespeare.

Sir Nicholas Bacon died in 1579 and Francis returned from the court of France. He was then eighteen years of age, and he reluctantly entered Gray's Inn. About this time he had as his tutor in Italian John Florio who taught Italian to many prominent persons. Florio was the teacher of both French and Italian at the University of Oxford.

Both John Florio and his father, Michaelangelo Florio, were authors and it is probable that the elder Florio brought Italian books with him when he fled from Italy to escape persecution because he was a Protestant. As he was interested in play-writing he undoubtedly had in his library the Italian books which his son could have used when tutoring Francis Bacon. For instance, Giambattista Giraldi (1504-1573), one of the important dramatists of Ferrara, Northern Italy, wrote *Epitia,* from which Shakespeare's *Measure for Measure* derives. His *Moor of Venice* became the basis of Shakespeare's *Othello,* and *Pecorone,* by Ser Giovanni Fiorentino, was the source of *The Merchant of Venice.* John Florio translated into English some of his father's plays, one of which, *Tanto Traffico Per Nienti* (Considerable Movement For Nothing) closely resembles Shakespeare's *Much Ado About Nothing* in its title.

The French life of Bacon was published in 1631, five years after his death on Easter Sunday, 1626. This Life says that Bacon traveled extensively on the Continent, not only in France but also in Spain and Italy. This may explain why so many of the Shakespeare plays have Italian settings. For in addition to the three plays mentioned above eight more have their action in Italy. Those in the Roman Forum include *Julius Ceasar, Anthony and Cleopatria, Cymbeline, Corolanus* and *Titus Andronicus. Romeo and Juliet* is laid in Verona; *Much Ado About Nothing* in Messina, Sicily: *Cymbeline,* partly in Italy and partly in Britain.

The art of concealment or veiled allusion is often to be noticed in letters. Sir Tobie Matthew was Bacon's closest friend. In a letter to Francis, Sir Tobie wrote; "I will not presume to return you weight for weight, but measure for measure". Had he been reading the manuscript of the Play, *Measure for Measure?* We know that Bacon wrote to Sir Tobie Mathew: "my head being then wholly employed about invention" referring to the Elizabethan word for poetry. In another letter Bacon told Sir Tobie "to be careful of the writings submitted to you, that no man may see them."

Sir Tobie Matthew replied to Bacon on some other occasion of doubtless similar nature, around the time that the First Folio came out: — "The most prodigious wit that ever I knew of my nation, and of this side of the sea, is of your Lordship's name though he be known by another." If Sir Tobie Matthew was referring to Bacon's acknowledged works, the essays, etc., this expression "the most prodigious wit — (mind), "might well apply, but when he adds "of your Lordship's name, though he be known by another" we may be sure that he knew that

Bacon also wrote under another name.

Bacon himself acknowledged being a concealed poet in a letter to John Davies, author of *Nosce Tiepsum,* who afterwards became attorney-general for Ireland. The last line of the letter reads: "So desiring you to be good to concealed poets, I continue your very assured, Fr. Bacon. Gray's Inn, this 28 March, 1603".

Sir Tobie Matthew's words reflect the spirit of the Elizabethan times. This was a period of veiled allusions, of finding ways of including in a letter or a conversation a casual reference, an incidental mention of something, either directly or by implication which could mean nothing to one person or be of the utmost importance to another. The age is full of examples of authors concealing their authorship in Latin anagrams on the title pages of their works or of writing letters, as Lady Ann Bacon did, in perfectly good English but using only Greek letters!

We have seen in an earlier chapter how the satirists, Marston and Hall, did their best to expose what they believed to be the truth about the authorship of some of the first Plays ascribed to Shakespere by writing a series of rather remarkable satires.

Ben Jonson said in his *Discoveries:* "My conceit of his Person was never increased toward him, by his place or honors. But I have, and doe reverence him for the greatness, which was only proper to himselfe, in that hee seem'd to mee ever, by his worke one of the greatest men, and most worthy of admiration, that had beene in many ages. In his adversity I ever prayed, that God would give him strength; for Greatness hee could not want. Neither could I condole in a word, or syllable for him as knowing no Accident could doe harme to virtue; but rather help to make it manifest." (fig. 28)

In another quotation, Ben Jonson gives a picture of

102 *Discoveries.*

affections more in his power. The feare of every man that heard him, was, lest hee should make an end.

*Scriptorum Catalogus.* *Cicero* is said to bee the only wit, that the people of *Rome* had equall'd to their *Empire. Ingenium par imperio.* We have had many, and in their severall Ages, (to take in but the former *Seculum.*) *Sir Thomas Moore*, the elder *Wiat*, *Henry*, Earle of *Surrey*; *Chaloner*, *Smith*, *Cliot*, B.*Gardiner*, were for their times admirable: and the more, because they began Eloquence with us. Sir *Nico: Bacon*, was singular, and almost alone, in the beginning of Queene *Elizabeths* times. Sir *Philip Sidney*, and Mr. *Hooker* (in different matter) grew great Masters of wit, and language; and in whom all vigour of Invention, and strength of judgement met. The Earle of *Essex*, noble and high; and Sir *Walter Rawleigh*, not to be contemn'd, either for judgement, or stile. Sir *Henry Savile* grave, and truly letter'd; Sir *Edwin Sandes*, excellent in both: Lo: *Egerton*, the Chancellor, a grave, and great Orator; and best, when hee was provok'd. But his learned, and able (though unfortunate) *Successor*) is he, who hath fill'd up all numbers, and perform'd that in our tongue, which may be compar'd, or preferr'd, either to insolent *Greece*, or haughty *Rome*. In short, within his view, and about his times, were all the wits borne, that could honour a language, or helpe study. Now things daily fall: wits grow downe-ward, and *Eloquence* growes back-ward: So that hee may be nam'd, and stand as the *marke*, and ακμη of our language.

(Margin: Sir *Thomas Moore.* Sir *Thomas Wiat.* *Hen: Earle of Surrey.* Sir *Thomas Cheloner.* Sir *Thomas Smith.* Sir *Thomas Cliot.* *B. Gardiner.* Sir *Nic: Bacon.* L.K. Sir *Philip Sydney.* M. *Richard Hooker.* *Rob. Earle of Essex.* Sir *Walter Raleigh.* Sir *Henry Savile.* Sir *Edwin Sands.* Sir *Thomas Egerton.* L.C. Sir *Francis Bacon,* L.C.)

*I have* ever observ'd it, to have beene the office of a wise Patriot, among the greatest affaires of the *State*, to take care of the *Common-wealth* of Learning. For Schooles, they are the *Seminaries* of State: and nothing is worthier the study of a States-man, then that part of the *Republicke*, which wee call the *advancement* of Letters. Witnesse the care of *Iulius Cæsar*; who in the heat of the civill warre, writ his bookes of *Analogie*, and dedicated them to *Tully*. This made the late Lord S. *Albane*, entitle his worke, *novum Organum*. Which though by the most of superficiall men; who cannot get beyond the Title of *Nominals*, it is not penetrated, nor understood: it really openeth all defects of Learning, whatsoever; and is a Booke.

(Margin: *De Augmentis scientiarum.* *Iulius Cæsar.* Lord S. *Albane.* *Horat: de art: Poetica.* *De corrupta morum.*)

*Qui longum noto scriptori porriget ævum.*

My conceit of his Person was never increased toward him, by his place, or honours. But I have, and doe reverence him for the greatnesse, that was onely proper to himselfe, in that hee seem'd to mee ever, by his worke one of the greatest men, and most worthy of admiration, that had beene in many Ages. In his adversity I ever prayed, that *God* would give him strength: for *Greatnesse* hee could not want. Neither could I condole in a word, or syllable for him; as knowing no Accident could doe harme to vertue; but rather helpe to make it manifest.

Fig. 28 *Discoveries* by Ben Jonson.

Bacon somewhat different from that held by most persons. "There happened in my time one noble speaker who was full of gravity in his speaking. His language where he could spare or pass by a jest was nobly censorious. No man ever spoke more neatly, more pressly, more weightily, or suffered less emptiness, less idleness, in what he uttered. No member of his speach but consisted of his own graces.

"His hearers could not cough or look aside from him without loss. He commanded where he spoke, and had his Judges angry and pleased at his devotion. No man had their affections (i.e. emotions) more in his power. The fear of every man who heard him was lest he should make an end."[3]

A friend, John Davies, of Herford, wrote in 1610 a sugared sonnet to Francis Bacon. It was not unusual in those days for literary men to send one another complimentary sonnets written in sugared ink so that the writing would shine. These were not intended for publication but this example by John Davies has survived, and as it is practically unknown, it is reproduced here.

To the royall, ingenious and all-learned Knight Sir Francis Bacon.

> Thy bounty and the Beauty of thy Witt
> Comprised in Lists of Law and learned Arts,
> Each making thee for great implovment fitt
> Which now thou hast (though short of thy deserts)
> Compells my pen to let fall shining Inke
> And to bedew the Baies that deck thy Front;
> And to thy health in Helicon to drinke
> As to her Bellamour the Muse is wont;
> For thou dost her embozom, and dost use
> Her company for sport twixt grave affairs;
> So utterest Law the livelyer through thy Muse.
> And for that all thy Notes are sweetest Aires,
> My muse thus notes thy worth in every line
> With yncke which thus she sugers so to shine.

Sir Tobie Matthew, Bacon's friend, wrote, "I never saw in him any trace of a vindictive mind . . . never heard him utter a word to any man's disadvantage, from personal feeling . . . it is not his greatness that I admire but his virtue; it is not the favors that I have received from him — infinite though they be — but it is his whole life and character that have thus enthralled and enchained my heart." And again Sir Tobie Matthew wrote of Bacon, "A man so rare in knowledge of so many severall kinds, endued with the faculty and felicity of expressing it all in so elegant, significant, so abundant and yet so choice and ravishing a way of words, of metaphor and allusions as perhaps the world hath not seen since it was a world. I know this may seem a great Hyperbole, and strange kind of riotous excess of speech; but the best means of putting to shame will be for you to place any other man of yours by this of mine."

The Rev. William Rawley, Bacon's Chaplain and secretary, who was also Chaplain to James I and Charles I, wrote of Bacon; — "I have been induced to think; That if there were a Beame of Knowledge, derived from God, upon any Man, in these modern Times, it was upon Him. For though he was a great Reader of Books; yet he had not his Knowledge from Books; but from some Grounds and Notions, from within himself. Which, notwithstanding he vented with great caution, and circumspection."

William Hepworth Dixon, noted author and biographer (1821-1879), law student in the Inner Temple and later Magistrate for Middlesex, says, in his *Personal History of Lord Bacon:* — "The attempt to overthrow some of his judgements fail. Of the thousands of decisions pronounced by him, the ferret eye of Coke, Bacon's great enemy, when Francis Bacon is lying helpless beneath his feet, cannot drag one to light that has the ghost of a chance of being proved corrupt or a declaration that a wrong verdict has been pronounced. Not one is reversed."

Another jurist, Judge Thomas Webb, Regius Professor of Law at the University of Dublin, wrote in *The Mystery of William Shakespeare,* 1902:- "If anything is certain in regard to the sonnets, the poems and the plays (of Shakespeare) it is that the author was a lawyer."

Sir James Wilde, K.C., afterwards Lord Penzance, remarked on "Shakespeare's perfect familiarity with not only the principals, axioms and maxims, but the technicalities of English law, a knowledge so perfect and intimate that he was never incorrect and never at fault."

The American lawyer, Franklin Fiske Heard, author of the *Legal Acquirements of Wm. Shakespeare,* (1867) and *Shakespeare as a Lawyer,* (1883) declared that:- "*The Comedy of Errors* shows that Shakespeare was very familiar with some of the most refined principals of the science of special pleading, a science which contains the quintessence of the law ... In the second part of Henry IV, Act 5, Scene v, Pistol uses the term *absque hoc,* which is technical in the last degree. This was a species of traverse ... the sublety of its texture and the total dearth of explanation in all the reports and treatises in the time of Shakespeare with respect to its principals, seem to justify the conclusion that he must have attained a knowledge of it from actual practice." In addition we find that there are, by actual count, over 600 different legal terms in the sonnets, plays and poems, "all brought into the text so naturally and unobstrusively that the lay reader scarcely notices them, whilst the legal mind notes with astonishment their correct use. The cumulative evidence that a practising lawyer wrote the plays becomes overwhelming."[4]

If William Shakspere of Stratford-on-Avon had possessed the legal knowledge demonstrated in the plays surely he would not have failed to bequeath in his will his valuable literary works. This will, which has been preserved, itemizes the disposition of his effects in detail. Seventeen of the plays and the sonnets had been printed before his death in 1616. Are we to believe that the world's greatest literary genius did not have in his possession a single copy of any of them, either in print or in manuscript? He does not mention them in his will nor does he mention a single book. Books were valuable in those days and they certainly should have been mentioned in a will that contained three pages and listed so many household effects.

This will was in the hand writing of Francis Collins, the Warwick solicitor. Shakspere signed each page, each signature having a different spelling. (fig. 4) The handwriting also differs and is of poor quality. The excuse has been offered, by way of explanation, that he was ill at the time of signing his Will and therefore could not write properly. This does not hold because the earlier signatures written when he was in good health are even worse and again differ from each other in spelling.

Shakspere's daughter, Mrs. Susanna Hall, inherited his house, New Place. Mrs. Hall was able to sign her own name after she was married to Dr. Hall. But before that, like her sister Judith, she had to make her 'mark' (a cross) when signing a document.

Is it not astonishing that a man who had one of the largest vocabularies of any Englishman, -17,677 words,[5] and who had written in Henry VI; -"Ignorance is the curse of God,- Knowledge the wing wherewith we fly to heaven", - a man who over and over again extolled knowledge and deplored ignorance, should have so neglected the education of his daughters that they could not even sign their names?

*Lectori S.*

QVod præcipuum ſibi duxit *Honoratiſſimus Dominus* meus, *Vice-Comes Sancti Albani*, *Academiis*, & viris literatioribus ut Cordi eſſet, id (credo) obtinuit; quandoquidem inſignia hæc Amoris & Mœſtitiæ Monumenta indicant, quantū Amiſsio ejus eorundem Cordi doleat. Neq; verò parcâ manu Symbolum hoc conjecerunt in eum *Muſæ*; (plurimos enim, eóſq; optimos Verſus apud me contineo;) ſed quia ipſe mole non delectabatur, Molem haud magnam extruxi. Satis eti-

A 2 am

Fig. 29 Rawley's Preface to *Manes Verulamiani* and translation.

## *Chapter VIII*
## *Mr. Francis Bacon of Tribute or Giving What is Dew*[1]

BOUT a month after Bacon's death on Easter Sunday, 9 April 1626, clearer and more numerous allusions were made to his fame as a *poet* in the wonderful series of thirty-two eulogies written in Latin and published in May, 1626, by Dr. William Rawley under the title of *Manes Verulamiani.* (Shades of Verulam, from Francis Bacon's title, Baron of Verulam').[2]

An original edition of this little book of eulogies, which is very rare, is listed in the British Museum under the title, "Memoriae Honoratissimi Domini Francisci, Baronis de Verulamio, Vice-comitis Sancti Albani Sacrum, Londini in Officina Johannis Haviland 1626."[3] The translation used is by Father William A. Sutton, S. J.

In his short Preface Dr. Sutton says: "... The poems are full proof that a large number of contemporaneous scholars, Fellows of the Universities and members of the Inns of Court, knew Bacon to be a supreme poet. In the fourth poem he gets credit for uniting philosophy to the drama, for restoring philosophy through comedy and tragedy. Other equally amazing titles to literary fame are also lavished on him in many places throughout the series . . ."

Dr. Sutton then translates W. Rawley's Preface to the collection of tributes to Bacon (fig. 29)

> "To the Reader Greeting.
> What my Lord the Right Honourable Viscount St. Albans valued most, that he should be dear to seats of learning and to men of letters, that (I believe) he has secured; since these tokens of love and memorials of sorrow prove how much his loss grieves their heart. And indeed with no stinted hand have the Muses bestowed upon him this emblem (for very many poems, and the best too, I withhold from publication); but since he himself delighted not in quantity, no great quantity have I put forth. Moreover let it suffice to have laid, as it were, these foundations in the name of the present age; this fabric (I think) every age will embellish and enlarge; but to what age it is given to put the last touch, that is known to God only and the fates." W. Rawley, S. T. D.

Thomas Randolph, of Trinity College, writes: (No. 32)

> " . . . When he perceived that the arts were held by no roots, and like seed scattered on the surface of the soil were withering away, he taught the Pegasean arts (i.e., poetic arts) to grow, as grew the spear of Quirinus swiftly into a laurel tree. Therefore since he taught the Heliconian goddesses to flourish no lapse of ages shall dim his glory. The ardour of his noble heart could bear no longer that you, divine Minerva, should be despised. His godlike pen restored your wonted honour . . . Pallas too, now arrayed in a new robe, paces forth . . ."

Another writer refers to his tremendous literary output (No. 24) " . . . You have filled the world with your writing and the ages with your fame . . ." C. D., Kings College.

No. 13:

> " . . . But she (Nature) says, 'Stay your advance and

**13.** ***On the Death of the Right Honourable Lord, Francis Viscount St. Albans, Baron Verulam, a Peerless Man.***

Forbear: our woe loves eloquent silence, since he has died who alone could speak, could speak what the chivalrous ring of princes were lost in admiration at, and (who alone could) resolve the intricacies of the law in the case of anxious defendants. A mighty work. But Verulam restores too our ancient arts and founds new ones. Not the same way as our predecessors; but he with fearless genius challenges the deepest recesses of nature. But she says, "Stay your advance and leave to posterity what will delight the coming ages to discover. Let it suffice for our times, that being ennobled by your discoveries they should glory in your genius. Something there is, which the next age will glory in; something there is, which it is fit should be known to me alone: let it be your commendation to have outlined the frame with fair limbs, for which no one can wholly perfect the members: thus his unfinished work commends the artist Apelles, since no hand can finish the rest of his Venus. Nature having thus spoken and yielding to her blind frenzy cut short together the thread of his life and work. But you, who dare to finish the weaving of this hanging web, will alone know whom these memorials hide."

H. T., Fellow of Trinity College

Fig. 30 Tribute no. 13 translation.

leave to posterity what will delight the coming ages to discover. Let it suffice for our times, that being ennobled by your discoveries they should glory in your genius. Something there is, which the next age will glory in; something there is, which it is fit should be known to me alone: . . .But you, who dare to finish the weaving of this hanging web, will alone know whom these memorials hide.'" H. T., Fellow of Trinity College. (fig. 30)

No. 7, by T. Vincent, Trinity College.

"Some there are though dead live in marble, and trust all their duration to long lasting columns; others shine in bronze, or are beheld in yellow gold, and deceiving themselves think they deceive the fates. Another division of men surviving in a numerous offspring, like Niobe irreverent, despise the mighty gods; but your fame adheres not to sculptured columns, nor is read on the tomb Stay traveller, your steps . . ." (fig. 31)

"Stay Passenger, why goest thou by so fast", is found on the Shakespeare monument at Stratford. The American College Dictionary defines passenger as 'a traveler'. Thus T. Vincent cleverly drew attention to this particular line to show Bacon's connection with the Shakespeare Plays. He uses the Latin phrase, 'siste viator iter' E. A. Andrews, L. L. D., in his *Copius and Critical Latin-English Lexicon* translates these words as follows: "Siste, stay; viator, a traveller; and iter, a going by."

No. 4 (Translated by W. E. Rand)

" . . . so did Philosophy, involved in scholar's riddles, call Bacon to her rescue; so by his touch entranced, she reared her crest; and as she crept along the ground in comic sock, he did not succour her with some devise that gossips would approve, but made her wholly new. Then with more polished art, he rose in higher buskin, and the Stagerite,[4] another Virbius, lives again in a new Organon." R. P.

This passage may seem obscure but actually is quite clear and direct, making allowance for the Elizabethan manner of speech among scholars. It traces in the plays

7. *To The Same.*

Some there are though dead live in marble, and trust all their duration to long lasting columns; others shine in bronze, or are beheld in yellow gold, and deceiving themselves think they deceive the fates. Another division of men surviving in a numerous offspring, like Niobe[13] irreverent, despise the mighty gods; but your fame adheres not to sculptured columns, nor is read on the tomb (with) "Stay, traveller, your steps"; if any progeny recalls their sire, not of the body is it, but born, so to speak, of the brain, as Minerva from Jove's: first your virtue provides you with an ever-lasting monument, your books another not soon to collapse, a third your nobility; let the fates now celebrate their triumphs, who having nothing yours, Francis, but your corpse. Your mind and good report, the better parts survive; you have nothing of so little value as to ransom the vile body withal.

T. Vincent, Trinity College.

Fig. 31 Tribute no. 8 translation.

the course of Philosophy, first creeping in Comedy in socks, "a light shoe worn by the classic actors of comedy", then rising in buskin to tragedy, because the buskin was "a kind of half-boot or high shoe reaching to the middle calf, worn by ancient actors in tragedy to increase their height", and finally ending to live again in the *Novum Organum,* Bacon's great prose work.

Now this combining of philosophy with comedy and tragedy reaches its peak in the Shakespeare plays, whose *publication dates* show that, omitting the histories, the comedies came before the tragedies, with two exceptions: *Titus Andronicus,* 1594, and *Romeo and Juliet,* 1597. Therefore the chronology of the author of this eulogy is substantially correct.

One of the eulogies (No. 18) tells how *Melpomene, Muse of Tragedy,* grieved over Bacon's death. (fig. 32)

> "The Day star of the Muses has fallen ere his time! Fallen, ah me, is the very care and sorrow of the Clarian god (Phoebus Apolo), 'thy darling, Nature, and the world's — Bacon: aye — passing strange — the grief of very Death. What privilege did not the cruel destiny claim? Death would fain spare, and yet she could not. *Melpomene,* chiding, would not suffer it, and spake these words to the stern goodess: 'Never was *Atropos* truly heartless before now; keep thou all the world, only give me Phoebus back.' " *Anonymous.*

Why did *Melpomene,* muse of tragedy grieve so excessively unless it was because she knew that Bacon was the author of the great Shakespeare tragedies?

In the 20th eulogy there is a reference to another Muse: (fig. 33) "Weep ye now truly, *Clio,* and *Clio's* sisters." Anonymous.

Just as *Melpomene,* Muse of Tragedy, is sorrowing, so now *Clio,* Muse of History, and her sister muses as well,

**XVIII**

***On the Death of the Most Cultured, and, too, Most Noble Man, Francis Lord Verulam, Viscount St. Alban.[1]***

**The Day star of the Muses hath fallen ere his time! Fallen ah me, is the very care and sorrow of the Clarian god,[2] thy darling, Nature, and the world's — Bacon: aye — passing strange — the grief of very Death. What privilege did not the cruel Destiny[3] claim? Death would fain spare, and yet she would it not. Melpomene, chiding, would not suffer it, and spake these words to the stern goddesses: "Never was Atropos truly heartless before now; keep thou all the world, only give my Phœbus back." Ah me, alas! nor Heaven nor Death nor the Muse, oh Bacon, nor my prayers could bar the fates.**

Fig. 32 Tribute no. 18 translation.

are grieving for him. Surely this lamentation of *Clio* is called forth because of the 10 historical plays of Shakespeare and not merely by the *History of Henry VII,* the only historical prose work bearing Francis Bacon's name.

Also, in the next line of the 20th eulogy, there is a significant reference: "Ah fallen is the tenth Muse, the glory of the choir."

XX

*In Obitum ejusdem, &c.*

Si nisi qui dignus, nemo tua fata (BACONE)
Fleret, erit nullus, credito nullus erit.

Plangite jam verè *Clio*, *Cliûsque* sorores,
Ah decima occubuit musa, decusque chori.

Ah nunquam verè infælix priùs ipsus *Apollo!*
Unde illi qui sic illum amet alter erit?

Ah numerum non est habiturus; jamque necesse est,
Contentus musis ut sit *Apollo* novem.

XX

*On the Death of the Same, etc.*

If only the worthy, Bacon, shall lament thy fate, ah none will do it, there'll be none, believe me, there'll be none.

Weep ye now truly, Clio, and Clio's sisters.[1] Ah, fallen is the tenth Muse, the glory of the choir. Ah never really was Apollo himself unhappy before! When shall he ever gain another so to love him? Ah me! the full number he shall have no more: now must Apollo be content with nine Muses.

[1] This poet seems to have been reading Ovid's *Art of Love*, i. 27, *Clio Cliusque sorores*.

Fig. 33 Tribute no. 20 translation.

This is a most important disclosure and it is echoed in the 2nd eulogy by S. Collins, R. C. P., Regius Professor of Divinity at Cambridge, who says that Bacon was "A muse more rare than the nine Muses." (Sutton translation). In other words a tenth muse.

It was significant to find that in the 38th Sonnet Shakespeare elevates his muse to the rank of a tenth muse "ten times more in worth than those old nine which rimers invocate."

*SONNET XXXVIII*

How can my Muse want subject to invent,
While thou dost breathe, that pour'st into my verse
Thine own sweet argument, too excellent
For every vulgar paper to rehearse?
O! give thyself the thanks, if aught in me
Worthy perusal stand against thy sight;
For who's so dumb that cannot write to thee,
When thou thyself dost give invention light?
Be thou the tenth Muse, ten times more in worth
Than those old nine which rimers invocate;
And he that calls on thee, let him bring forth
Eternal numbers to outlive long date.
If my slight Muse do please these curious days,
The pain be mine, but thine shall be the praise.

The words *invent, invention* and *numbers,* meant, in Elizabethan times, composing verses, poetry and poems.

Having found that Shakespeare had referred to the tenth muse as his inspiration and that several of the writers of tributes to Bacon called *him* a tenth muse, this confusion had to be cleared up. The eulogists indicated that it was Bacon himself. But this seemed absurd, for the muses were all women. Perhaps the writers were speaking of Francis Bacon's *nom de plume?* Perhaps they went as far as they dared in revealing his secret name? If evidence could be found that Bacon had been dissatisfied with the idea of selecting his muse from one of the nine classical muses and had chosen another female entity as being more appropriate to represent his ideals, aspirations, and activities, and if her name could be found, the mystery might then be cleared up and the key to his *nom de plume* revealed.

Fortunately this evidence exists in several places. First in a poem, preserved in the Archepiscopal Library

**A Monsieur Francois Bacon**

**Sonnett**

Ce qu'inspiré du Ciel, et plein d'affection
Je comble si souvent ma bouche, et ma poitrine
Du sacré Nom fameus de ta Royne divine
Ses valeurs en sont cause et sa perfection
Si ce siècle de fer si mainte Nation
Ingratte à ses honneurs, n'avait l'ame Æmantine:
Ravis de ce beau Nom, qu'aus Graces je destine
Avec eus nous l'aurions en admiration.
Donc (Baccon) s'il advient que ma Muse l'on vante
Ce n'est pas qu'elle soit ou diserte, ou sçavante:
Bien que *vostre Pallas* me rende mieus instruit
C'est pource que mon Lut chant sa gloire sainte
Ou qu'en ces vers nayfz son Image est empraînte:
Ou que ta vertu claire en mon ombre reluit.

—La Jessée.

Jean de la Jessée, secretaire de la chambre to Francis, Duke of Anjou, published in 1582 at Antwerp, Sonnets [etc.?] to friends and patrons, 4 vols. Qo. Begley says that from its position in the bound-up volumes of Anthony Bacon's MSS. the above sonnet seems to have been written about 1595, or 1596. It was not published before its appearance in *Is it Shakespeare?* Begley calls attention to the words *vostre Pallas,* and compares with Philautia's speech in Essex's *Device* of 1595, which was furnished with marginal notes by Francis Bacon for Essex's eye. Essex was credited with the *Device* until the discovery of the MSS. showed who was the author. [*Gibson Papers,* Vol V. No. 118, MS. volumes.]

Fig. 34 *A Sonnett* by la Jessée.

*Virgidemiarum. Lib. 6.* 93

SAT. I.

He can implore the heathen Deities,
To guide his bold and busy enterprise;
Or filch whole Pages at a clap for need
From honest *Petrarch*, clad in English weed;
While big *But Ohs* each stanzae can begin,
Whose trunke and tayle sluttish and hartlesse bin;
He knowes the grace of that new elegance,
Which sweet *Philisides* fetch't of late from *France*,
That well beseem'd his high-stil'd *Arcady*,
Tho others marre it with much liberty;
In Epithets to ioyne two words in one,
Forsooth for Adiectiues cannot stand alone,
As a great Poet could of *Bacchus* say,
That he was *Semele-femori-gena*.
Lastly he names the spirit of *Astrophell*,
Now hath not *Labeo* done wondrous well?
But ere his Muse her weapon learne to weild.

Or

Fig. 35 *Satire I* by Joseph Hall.

at Lambeth Palace, London, originally found among Anthony Bacon's papers and manuscripts. It had been written to his brother, Francis, by the French poet, Jean de la Jessée about 1595 or 1596. The eleventh line reveals the name of Bacon's Muse. (fig. 34)

*Sonnett'*

"Donc (Baccon) s'il advient que ma Muse l'on vante;
Ce n'est pas qu'elle soit ou diserte, ou scavante;
Bien que *vostre Pallas* me rende mieus instruit
C'est pource que mon Lute chant sa gloire sainte
Ou qu'en ces vers nayfz son Image est emprainte:
Ou que ta vertu claire en mon ombre reluit".
La Jessée'

La Jessée is comparing muses and says that he thinks that his own muse is lacking in elequence as compared with Bacon's *Pallas (vostre Pallas,* your Pallas) who had, however, instructed him to do better. The important point is that a French poet who knew Bacon intimately enough to address a 'Sonnett' to him was familiar with the fact that *Pallas Athene* was Bacon's Muse.

We have seen that the name, *Labeo* was used by Marston and Hall to represent Bacon. In this satire *Labeo* has a muse with a weapon and we know that Pallas is always shown with her weapon, a spear. Evidently Joseph Hall had penetrated this secret too, for he says in his *Virgidemiarus,* Lib. 6, page 93 Sat. I (fig. 35):

"He can implore the heathen Deities,
To guide his bold and busy enterprise;
. . . . . . . . . . . . . . . . . . . . . . . . . . . . . . . . . . . . . .
Now hath not *Labeo* done wondrous well?
But ere his Muse her weapon learned to wield."

*Pallas Athene,* (fig. 36) as we know, was the national divinity of the Greeks and her Latin name was *Minerva.* She was the protector of the State, the goddess of wisdom and knowledge, poetry, drama and the fine arts. Her bronze statue 30 feet in height, by Pheidias, stood on the Acropolis. According to Pausanis i. 28, the gleam of her helmet and spear could be seen by the mariners approaching from Sunium. The name Pallas was derived

Fig. 36 Pallas Athene with helmut, spear and goat skin breastplate. The Serpent of Ignorance lies at her feet.

from *to shake,* and according to the Greek Classical Lexicon she was known to the Greeks as the "Brandisher of the Spear." Her helmet was supposed to confer invisibility at will (Knights of the Helmet of Gray's Inn!) and her shield and breast-plate were made of goat skin, for the goat was sacred to the drama, the word 'goat' combined with the verb 'to sing', forming *tragedy,* or literally, 'goatsong'.

Servius, the commentator on Virgil's *Aenied,* 1.43, tells us that "*Pallas* was wont to shake her spear."

SHAKE (her) SPEAR (e); SHAKE-SPEARE! Bacon's nom de plume derived from his tenth muse, Pallas!

Shake-speare, with the hyphen, was used on the title page of the first quarto of Hamlet 1603 (fig. 49), King Lear, 1608 (fig. 46) and the Sonnets, 1609 (fig. 42).

The hyphenated spelling of the name was never used by the actor of Stratford-on-Avon, nor by any member of his family. Sir Edmund K. Chambers collected eighty-three variations in the spelling of the name in England (whether or not related to the Stratford man), the large majority of which phonetically require the short "a." Not one of these eighty-three variations hyphenated the two syllables into the artificial-looking name, Shake-Speare.

The many attributes of Pallas Athene corresponded closely with Bacon's manifold activities and broad ideals. Each of the nine muses limited her field of inspiration to one of the specific arts. Concerning wisdom and knowledge, over which Pallas presided, we know of Bacon's deep interest in these from his works and from the letter he wrote in 1591 to his uncle, Lord Burleigh, in which he said:

> " . . . I confess that I have as vast contemplative ends, as I have moderate civil ends: for I have taken all knowledge to be my province; and if I could purge it of two

sorts of rovers, whereof the one with frivolous disputations, confutations, and verbosities: the other with blind experiments and aricular traditions and impostures, hath committed so many spoils; I hope I should bring in industrious observations, grounded conclusions, and profitable inventions and discoveries; the best state of that province. This, whether it be curiosity, or vain glory, or nature, or if one take it favorably, *philanthropia,* is so fixed in my mind, as it cannot be removed . . . I will become . . . a true pioneer in that mine of truth, which he (anaxagoras) said, lay so deep." (Francis Bacon, from my lodging at Gray's Inn).

That he accomplished what he set out to do is acknowledged in Boswell's touching tribute, Sutton's translation: (No. 5)

"He hath left the living, whom alone it was wont to bear the laurel crown for. Verulam (from Bacon's title, Baron of Verulam) reigning in the citadel of the gods shines with a golden crown . . . Than whom no inhabitant of Earth was master of greater intellectual gifts: nor does any survivor so skillfully unite *Themis* (goddess of Law) and *Pallas*. While he flourished the sacred choir of the Muses influenced by these arts poured forth all their eloquence left none for wailing." William Boswell. (fig. 37)

There is another direct reference to *Pallas* under her Latin name, Minerva, in the 9th eulogy by R. C. of Trinity College. The very wording of the dedication is extraordinary:

"IN OBITUM ILLUSTRISSIMI CLARISSIMIQ HEROIS, DOMINI
FRANCISCI BACONI, BARONIS DE VERULAMIO".

Sutton translates this: "A Threnody on the Death of the most illustrious and renowned personage, Sir Francis

5. *To the Memory and Merits of the Right Honourable Lord Francis, Lord Verulam and Viscount St. Albans.*

Wail with weeping turbulent streams sprung from beneath the hoof of Pegasus, and ye streams profane flow muddily with your current scarce dragging along the black dust.[11] And let the foliage of verdant Daphne falling from the hapless branches wither. Wherefore, ye Muses, would you cultivate the useless laurels of your sad garden? Nay, with stern axes cut down the trunk of the worthless tree. He hath left the living, whom alone it was wont to bear the laurel crown for. Verulam reigning in the citadel of the gods shines with a golden crown; and enthroned above the bounds of the sky he loves with face towards Earth to view the stars; who grudged the immortals that wisdom should be confined to the abode of the blessed, undertaking to bring it back and restore it to mortals by a new cult. Than whom no inhabitant of Earth was master of greater intellectual gifts; nor does any survivor so skilfully unite Themis and Pallas. While he flourished the sacred choir of the Muses influenced by these arts poured forth all their eloquence in his praise (and), left none for wailings

I, William Boswell
have laid (this offering on the tomb).

Fig. 37 Tribute no. 5 translation.

Bacon, Baron of Verulam". In looking up HEROIS it was found that this word meant more than *personage:* it meant also *demigoddess* or *heroine,* for, if the writer had employed the masculine form of the word, which is HEROS, it could have meant only a personage who was a *demigod* or *hero.* And when the writer called Bacon the 'precious gem of concealed literature' this was a great revelation.' For Bacon signed all of his works under his own name. Therefore the literature that was 'concealed' must have been written by him under a *nom de plume,* and as the eulogist clearly says that this literature was "composed by your genius and by *Minerva,"* it seemed clear that he is telling us that the *Minerva (Pallas* or Shake-speare) works were also written by Bacon! So now the feminine form — HEROIS — is explained: Bacon and his Muse, the goddess *Minerva,* are one and the same person. This makes it possible for the scholar, R. C., to correctly salute him with the feminine form, Herois, of the Latin word for Hero in the dedication, because he is addressing the *nom de plume* — the goddess *Minerva.* (No. 9, continued):

> "Muses pour forth your perennial waters in lamentations . . . The very nerve of genius, the marrow of persuasion, the golden stream of eloquence, the precious gem of concealed literature, the noble BACON, (ah! the relentless warp of the three sisters) has fallen by the fates. Oh how am I in verse like mine to commemorate you, sublime BACON! And those glorious memorials of all the ages composed by your genius and by *Minerva.* And with what learned, beautiful, profound matters the *Great Instauration* is full . . . "R. C., T. C." (Trinity College).

The *Great Instauration,* (i.e., The Great Restoration or Renovation of Knowledge) which is referred to in such glowing terms in this eulogy, was Bacon's greatest philosophical and scientific work. It was divided by him into six parts.

The fourth part, which, according to Spedding, has been "lost", was intended, as described by Bacon himself, to be his theatrical presentation of the interplay of the mental, emotional and moral nature of Man. He says: "I am forming a history and *Tabulae Inveniendi* for anger, fear, shame and the like, and matters political, and again for the operation of memory and judgment, not less than for heat or cold or light or vegetation."

Bacon goes on to say that historians and poets are the best instructors in this branch of human knowledge because in their works

> "we may find painted forth with great life how affections (emotions) are kindled and incited; how they disclose themselves, how they work, how they vary, how they gather and fortify and how they are enwrapped with one another."

He further explains in the second, or Latin, edition of the *Advancement of Learning* why historians and poets are best qualified to treat of human nature "because a man's character can be more powerfully delineated in action than in formal criticism".

Concerning dramatic poetry he says: "Its world is the theatre. It might be and aught to become of excellent use." He adds that unfortunately the theatre is too often used to corrupt and degrade instead of enlightening and elevating. Bacon deplores the corruption of the theatre in his day and the utter neglect of its power for instructing and improving. He reminds us that it was not so with the ancients, who made it the vehicle for improving men in virtue. "Wise men and great philosophers have thought it to be the plectrum of the mind, or as the bow is to the violin. For it is a secret of nature that men are more open to impressions in company than when alone."

Bacon was determined to keep his name out of the fourth part of *The Great Instauration*. He wrote: "I intend, yielding neither to my own personal aspiration or to the wishes of others, to keep steadily in view the success of this undertaking." In *The Interpretation of Nature* he says: "I am not hunting for fame nor establishing a sect. Indeed, to receive any private emolument from so great an undertaking I hold to be both ridiculous and base." He admonishes every one doing this work to do it, as he did "under a mask". The 1623 First Folio portrait shows a heavy line running from ear to chin which indi cates a mask. (fig. 1)

Bacon wanted the world ultimately to know the truth about the authorship of the plays written under his *nom de plume*. But he did not want to jeopardize the success of his greatest work by having his name connected with it while his enemies still lived. He seems to have hoped that, beginning with foreign countries, he would gradually emerge as the author of the fourth part of the *Great Instauration*. Writing in the draft of his will he says: "For my name and memory, I leave to men's charitable speeches and to foreign nations and the next ages; and to mine own countrymen after some time be passed."

This explains why his literary legatee, Dr. Wm. Rawley, first published in Latin his greatest hint about Bacon's connection with the theatre in two Dutch editions of Bacon's Life. These words do not appear in the English edition. "But what though the body be mortal, doubtless his memory and his work will live, and, in all probability, not perish, until all the theatrical machinery of this globe is dissolved." (fig. 38)

Although Francis Bacon kept his secret from the public, he did not keep it entirely to himself, for he needed

V I T A. 29

tis, & ſtudio incumbentis: una cum *Epitaphio*, quod lectiſſimus ille, & nitidioris ingenii, nec-non *Equeſtris Dignitatis* vir, *Henricus Wottonus*, Amoris & Admirationis ergo, compoſuit.

Quamvis autem *Corpus* quod depoſuit, *Mortale* fuerit, *Libri* tamen ejus, & *Memoria*, haud dubie perennes erunt; neque prius Fatis ceſſuri, quam *Orbis Terrarum Machina* diſſolvatur. Quo permotus, quantulacunque hæc, pro tenuitate mea, colligere viſum eſt, ut *Nomini* ejus in poſterum propagando quoquo modo inſervirem.

**GUIL. RAWLEY.**

Fig. 38 Rawley's Introduction to Bacon's *Opuscula*.

other literary men to help him. Ben Jonson was one of his 'good pens', as Bacon called his assistants. Jonson lived with Bacon at Gorhambury from 1618 until after the 1623 First Folio came out and he was listed as having received money in the household accounts in the year 1618. While serving Bacon as his secretary he translated some of Bacon's works into Latin and during this period he was also given the post of Master of the Court Revels and Licenser of Plays. This appointment came just two years prior to the publication of the First Folio. How ridiculous that Spedding should say "Shakespeare's plays, of which, though they had been filling the theatre for the last thirty years, I very much doubt whether Bacon had ever heard" — what nonsense, when Ben Jonson was living right in Bacon's house and taking an ac-

# To the memory of my beloued, The AVTHOR

## MR. WILLIAM SHAKESPEARE:

## AND what he hath left vs.

TO draw no enuy (Shakeſpeare) on thy name,
  Am I thus ample to thy Booke, and Fame:
While I confeſſe thy writings to be ſuch,
  As neither Man, nor Muſe, can praiſe too much.
'Tis true, and all mens ſuffrage. But theſe wayes
  Were not the paths I meant vnto thy praiſe:
For ſeelieſt Ignorance on theſe may light,
  Which, when it ſounds at beſt, but eccho's right;
Or blinde Affection, which doth ne're aduance
  The truth, but gropes, and vrgeth all by chance;
Or crafty Malice, might pretend this praiſe,
  And thinke to ruine, where it ſeem'd to raiſe.
Theſe are, as ſome infamous Baud, or Whore,
  Should praiſe a Matron. What could hurt her more?
But thou art proofe againſt them, and indeed
  Aboue th'ill fortune of them, or the need.
I, therefore will begin. Soule of the Age!
  The applauſe! delight! the wonder of our Stage!
My Shakeſpeare, riſe; I will not lodge thee by
  Chaucer, or Spenſer, or bid Beaumont lye
A little further, to make thee a roome:
  Thou art a Moniment, without a tombe,
And art aliue ſtill, while thy Booke doth liue,
  And we haue wits to read, and praiſe to giue.
That I not mixe thee ſo, my braine excuſes;
  I meane with great, but diſproportion'd Muſes:
For, if I thought my iudgement were of yeeres,
  I ſhould commit thee ſurely with thy peeres,
And tell, how farre thou didſtſt our Lily out-ſhine,
  Or ſporting Kid, or Marlowes mighty line.
And though thou hadſt ſmall Latine, and leſſe Greeke,
  From thence to honour thee, I would not ſeeke
For names; but call forth thund'ring Æſchilus,
  Euripides, and Sophocles to vs,
Paccuuius, Accius, him of Cordoua dead,
  To life againe, to heare thy Buskin tread,
And ſhake a Stage: Or, when thy Sockes were on,
  Leaue thee alone, for the compariſon

of

Of all, that inſolent Greece, or haughtie Rome
  ſent forth, or ſince did from their aſhes come.
Triumph, my Britaine, thou haſt one to ſhowe,
  To whom all Scenes of Europe homage owe.
He was not of an age, but for all time!
  And all the Muſes ſtill were in their prime,
When like Apollo he came forth to warme
  Our eares, or like a Mercury to charme!
Nature her ſelfe was proud of his deſignes,
  And ioy'd to weare the dreſsing of his lines!
Which were ſo richly ſpun, and wouen ſo fit,
  As, ſince, ſhe will vouchſafe no other Wit.
The merry Greeke, tart Ariſtophanes,
  Neat Terence, witty Plautus, now not pleaſe;
But antiquated, and deſerted lye
  As they were not of Natures family.
Yet muſt I not giue Nature all: Thy Art,
  My gentle Shakeſpeare, muſt enioy a part.
For though the Poets matter, Nature be,
  His Art doth giue the faſhion. And, that he,
Who caſts to write a liuing line, muſt ſweat,
  (ſuch as thine are) and ſtrike the ſecond heat
Vpon the Muſes anuile: turne the ſame,
  (And himſelfe with it) that he thinkes to frame;
Or for the lawrell, he may gaine a ſcorne,
  For a good Poet's made, as well as borne.
And ſuch wert thou. Looke how the fathers face
  Liues in his iſſue, euen ſo, the race
Of Shakeſpeares minde, and manners brightly ſhines
  In his well torned, and true-filed lines:
In each of which, he ſeemes to ſhake a Lance,
  As brandiſh't at the eyes of Ignorance.
Sweet Swan of Auon! what a ſight it were
  To ſee thee in our waters yet appeare,
And make thoſe flights vpon the bankes of Thames,
  That ſo did take Eliza, and our Iames!
But ſtay, I ſee thee in the Hemiſphere
  Aduanc'd, and made a Conſtellation there!
Shine forth, thou Starre of Poets, and with rage,
  Or influence, chide, or cheere the drooping Stage;
Which, ſince thy flight frō hence, hath mourn'd like night,
  And deſpaires day, but for thy Volumes light.

BEN: IONSON.

Fig. 39 Ben Jonson's second poem, First Folio.

tive part in the publication of the First Folio and also contributing two poems to it!

There was found recently in Francis Bacon's Library, now at Gorhambury, quarto copies of seven of Shakespeare's plays, including Hamlet, King Lear and Romeo and Juliet. They had been bound in with other pamphlets perhaps one hundred years ago. These are the earliest and the greatest number of Quarto editions of the Shakespeare plays which are in private possession in England. Bacon's silence about Shakespeare is more eloquent than words. Naturally he would not write about his own secret works or discuss his *nom de plume.*

The two poems that Ben Jonson contributed to the First Folio were, "To the Reader" (to be discussed later) and "To the Memory of my Beloved, the AUTHOR, Mr. William Shakespeare." (fig. 39). In the last named poem he makes two interesting references to the author. The first is:

> "In his well turned, and true filled lines,
> In each of which he seems to shake a lance,
> As brandish't at the eyes of Ignorance",

a reference that might well describe *Pallas Athene* whom the Greeks called "The brandisher of the Spear" and, the second:

> "Or when thy socks were on,
> Leave thee alone, for the comparison
> Of all that insolent Greece, or haughty Rome
> Sent forth or since did from their ashes come."

These four lines suddenly take on a special meaning when we find that they are the very words used by Ben Jonson in his *Discoveries,* Vol. II, 1641, p. 102 when describing Sir Francis Bacon, L. C. (Lord Chancellor):

> "But his learned and able (though unfortunate) Successor is he who hath filled up all numbers and performed that in our tongue, which may be Compar'd or preferr'd, either to insolent Greece or haughty Rome."
> (fig. 28)

Although Jonson was undoubtedly sworn to secrecy, it seems that he was doing his best, in his last work, to tell posterity, by repeating this extraordinary praise, almost word for word, that Francis Bacon and William Shakespeare were one and the same person.

And finally, as if to leave no doubt as to who was, in his opinion, the supreme master of the English language, Jonson continued in his Discoveries, p. 102:

> "Within his (Francis Bacon's) view, and about his times, were all the wits borne that could honour a language, or help study. Now things daily fall; wits grow downward, and Eloquance grows backward: So that he may be named, and stand as the Marke and Acme of our language." (fig. 28)

# *Chapter IX The Concealments Revealed*

ON the following pages are reproductions of the work sheets used by Jane Beckett to reveal the words concealed in various Shakespeare works, including the tombstone, the first quarto title pages, and the title page of the 1623 First Folio. The method she used to discover these words is explained in the first chapter. Several colors have been used to more clearly show the concealed words which include *Bacon, F, Fr, Francis, writ* and *poet.* The black letters indicate the frontwards spelling while the blue letters show the backwards spelling.

MR. WILLIAM

# SHAKESPEARES

COMEDIES,
HISTORIES, &
TRAGEDIES.

Publiſhed according to the True Originall Copies.

*LONDON*

Printed by Iſaac Iaggard, and Ed. Blount. 1623.

Fig. 1 Title page of the First Folio, 1623.

*Title Page, 1623 First Folio*

| 3 | M | 2 | R | 6 |  | I | V |  | V | T | I | N | L | U | L | O | I | L | A | B | M |  |  | D | S | E | H |  | A | D | K | N | E |
|---|---|---|---|---|---|---|---|---|---|---|---|---|---|---|---|---|---|---|---|---|---|---|---|---|---|---|---|---|---|---|---|---|---|
| A | S |  | P | D | E | R | A | A | R | G | E | G | S | A |  | J | C |  | O | C | M | A | E | A | D | S | I | I | E |  | S | Y |  |
| B | H |  | I | D | S | E | T | T | O | N | R | I | I | R | E | P | S |  |  | N | & | O |  | D | T | N | R | O | A | L | G |  | E |
| N | D | O | I | D | E | N | S | O |  | L | P |  | U | T | B | I | L | S | I | P | SH | L | E | U | D | C |  | S | A |  | C | T | C |
| U | O | O | R | H | D | S | I | E | N | O | G | R |  | D | T |  | O | N |  | I | T | T | H | R | E | A |  | M | T |  | R | S | U |
| E | E | I |  | P | O | O | R | C | I |  | G | L | I | L | N | A | A | N | L | I | L | G |  | I | C | R | O | O | P |  | I | E | E |
| U | S | R |  | T | M |  | A | E | R | H | T | T | I |  | N | O |  | T | D |  | R | G | O | N | E | I | S | D | H | R | O | O | U |
| C | T | C |  | A | S |  | C | D | U | E | L | HS | P | I | S | L | I | B | T | U |  | P | L |  | O | S | N | E | D | I | O | D | N |
| E |  | G | L | A | O | R | N | T | D |  | O | & | N |  |  | S | P | E | R | I | I | R | N | O | T | T | E | S | D | I |  | H | B |
|  | Y | S |  | E | I | I | S | D | A | E | A | M | C | O |  | C | J |  | A | S | G | E | G | R | A | A | R | E | D | P |  | S | A |
| E | N | K | D | A |  | H | E | S | D |  |  | M | B | A | L | I | O | L | U | L | N | I | T | V |  | V | I |  | 6 | R | 2 | M | 3 |

*Figure 40*

## *Tombstone Epitaph*

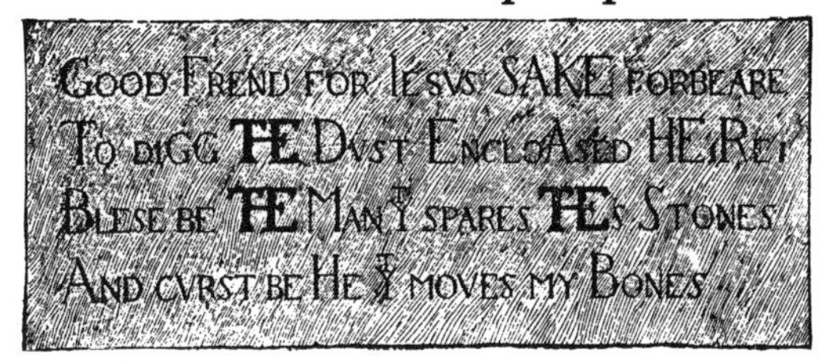


| . | G | S | O | E | O | N | D | O | . | B | F | . | R | Y | E | M | N | . | D | S | . | E | F | V | O | O | R | M | . | . | J | ty | E | . | S | E | U |
|---|---|---|---|---|---|---|---|---|---|---|---|---|---|---|---|---|---|---|---|---|---|---|---|---|---|---|---|---|---|---|---|---|---|---|---|---|---|
| H | S | . | . | E | S | B | A | . | K | T | E | S | . | R | F | U | O | C | R | . | B | D | E | N | A | A | R | . | E | S | . | E | T | N | O | O | . |
| T | D | S | I | . | G | S | G | TE | . | . | TE | S | . | E | D | R | U | A | S | P | T | S | . | . | E | ty | N | . | C | N | L | A | O | M | A | . | S |
| TE | E | . | D | E | . | B | H | . | E | E | . | S | R | E | E | L | . | B | B | . | L | E | E | R | S | . | E | E | . | H | B | . | E | D | . | E | TE |
| S | . | A | M | O | A | L | N | C | . | N | ty | E | . | . | S | T | P | S | A | U | R | D | E | . | S | TE | . | . | TE | G | S | G | . | I | S | D | T |
| . | O | O | N | T | E | . | S | E | . | R | A | A | N | E | D | B | . | R | C | O | U | F | R | . | S | E | T | K | . | A | B | S | E | . | . | S | H |
| U | E | S | . | E | ty | J | . | . | M | R | O | O | V | F | E | . | S | D | . | N | M | E | Y | R | . | F | B | . | O | D | N | O | E | O | S | G | . |

*Figure 41*

The strange poem, "To the Reader", by Ben Jonson, reminded me of the equally odd epitaph on the tombstone over Shakespeare's grave at Stratford-on-Avon. Both poems were in iambic verse, that is, having a foot of two syllables, one a short or unaccented, followed by a long or accented one. And in each poem every line has four iambi. I also remembered the story that was told about Shakspere and Jonson writing epitaphs together. And so I thought that it would be an interesting experiment to apply the 'double-it' method to the inscription on the *original* tombstone, especially so since it did not have Shakespeare's name on it nor the date of his birth or death to identify him.

After securing a copy of the original epitaph from the New York Public Library I found myself confronted with the problem of how to treat the three THE's which were tied together with a line that ran through the center, forming the 'H'. This was a kind of triple ligature. In addition there were two instances of a lower case t over a y. In my first trial I separated the capital letters of THE into their three component parts, allowing a space on my architect's paper for each letter. And I divided the ${}^{t}_{y}$ into two component parts, again placing each of these two letters in a square by itself. I worked for a long time on this arrangement and could get nothing out of it.

I had just about given up when the thought occurred to me that the three instances of the capital "THE", so obviously tied together with the horizontal line that not only connects them but forms the 'H', was meant to be counted as *one,* since they were fastened together as a unit and were unlike any other letters in the carving. As for the ${}^{t}_{y}$, since these two letters were placed *over* each other they might also be counted as a unit and occupy a single space together.

I was now ready for my second experiment. I began to count from every B to every A, from each C to each O and from O to N as described earlier. In less than half an hour from the time this new idea came to me I had found a perfect BACON in the exact center of the inscription on the tombstone with the additional letters F R adjoining it.

SHAKE-SPEARES

SONNETS.

Neuer before Imprinted.

---

---

AT LONDON

By *G.* *Eld* for *T.* *T.* and are
to be solde by *Iohn Wright*, dwelling
at Christ Church gate.
1609.

Fig. 42 *Shake-speares Sonnets,* first quarto, and concealment.

| + | + | + | + | . | S | 9 | H | O | A | 6 | K | I | E | . | – | E | S | T | P | A | E | G | A | . | R | H | E | C | S | R | . | V | S | H | O | C | N | . | N | T | E |
|---|---|---|---|---|---|---|---|---|---|---|---|---|---|---|---|---|---|---|---|---|---|---|---|---|---|---|---|---|---|---|---|---|---|---|---|---|---|---|---|---|---|
| S | T | I | S | R | . | H | N | C | E | . | V | T | E | A | R | . | . | G | B | N | E | I | F | L | O | L | R | E | E | W | . | D | I | . | M | T | P | H | R | G | I |
| I | N | R | T | W | E | . | D | N | . | H | A | O | T | J | . | . | L | Y | O | B | N | . | D | E | O | D | N | L | . | O | B | S | Y | . | . | E | G | B | . | . | E |
| O | L | T | D | . | . | E | F | R | O | A | R | . | . | D | T | N | . | A | T | . | . | T | A | . | N | T | D | . | . | R | A | O | R | F | E | . | . | D | T | L | O |
| E | . | . | B | G | E | . | . | Y | S | B | O | . | L | N | D | O | E | D | . | N | B | O | Y | L | . | . | J | T | O | A | H | . | N | D | . | E | W | T | R | N | I |
| I | G | R | H | P | T | M | . | I | D | . | W | E | E | R | L | O | L | F | I | E | N | B | G | . | . | R | A | E | T | V | . | E | C | N | H | . | R | S | I | T | S |
| E | T | N | . | N | C | O | H | S | U | . | R | S | C | E | H | R | . | A | G | E | A | P | T | S | E | – | . | E | I | K | 6 | A | O | H | 9 | S | . | + | + | + | + |

*Figure 42*

## King Lear

One of the most interesting first quarto title pages of the whole series of first quartos appeared in 1608. This was *King Lear,* which was published eight years after *Much Ado About Nothing.* The emphasis placed upon the author's name is startling. There is something odd even about the way the name is printed. It appears on the top line in huge type; "M. William Shak-speare:". Why, we may well ask is the 'r' of Mr. omitted. And why is the hyphenated form of the name, already familiar to us in *Hamlet* divided without an 'e' after the 'k'. There is room for the hyphen and the 'e' could have been placed there. And the exagerated emphasis upon the author's name is startling; we note its position on the top line and the size of the type used, remembering how, eight years previously, the name was put in the smallest possible type and almost lost in the middle of the title page of *Much Ado About Nothing.*

King Lear was one of the 'old plays' mentioned by Philip Henslowe in his Diary. But he places no author's name against it, large though it appeared in print on the first quarto title page. Nor does he mention any payment for it. Of course it may have been tried out prior to its publication, and was now therefore considered by him to be 'an old play.'

Queen Elizabeth having died in 1603 we note that, according to this title page King James now has his own company of actors and that although they usually played at the Globe on the Banke-side this edition is printed *"as it was played before the Kings Majestie at Whitehall upon* S. Stephans *night in Christmas Hollidayes".*

The text has 449 letters, 16 punctuation marks and the four digits of the date, which is used with the period that follows it.

M. William Shak-ſpeare:

*HIS*

True Chronicle Hiſtorie of the life and death of King LEAR and his three Daughters.

*With the vnfortunate life of* Edgar, *ſonne* and heire to the Earle of Gloſter, and his ſullen and aſſumed humor of TOM of Bedlam:

*As it was played before the Kings Maieſtie at Whitehall vpon* S. Stephans *night in Chriſtmas Hollidayes.*

By his Maieſties ſeruants playing vſually at the Gloabe on the Bancke-ſide.

*LONDON,*

Printed for *Nathaniel Butter,* and are to be ſold at his ſhop in *Pauls* Church-yard at the ſigne of the Pide Bull neere St. *Auſtins* Gate. 1608.

Fig. 43 *King Lear,* first quarto, and concealment.

# King Lear

| + | + | + | + | . | M | 8 | . | O | W | 6 | I | I | L | . | L | E | I | T | A | A | M | G | . | . | S | S | H |
|---|---|---|---|---|---|---|---|---|---|---|---|---|---|---|---|---|---|---|---|---|---|---|---|---|---|---|---|
| N | A | I | K | T | – | S | S | U | P | A | E | . | A | T | R | S | E | . | : | E | H | R | I | E | S | E | . |
| N | T | . | R | L | U | L | E | U | . | B | C | . | H | E | R | D | O | I | N | P | I | . | C | E | L | H | E |
| T | . | . | H | F | I | O | S | . | T | E | O | N | R | G | I | I | E | S | . | . | O | E | F | H | . | T | T |
| . | H | T | E | A | . | . | L | D | I | R | F | A | E | Y | . | – | A | H | N | C | D | R | . | U | D | H | E |
| C | A | . | T | S | H | L | . | U | O | A | F | P | . | . | K | N | I | I | N | . | G | P | . | O | L | H | E |
| S | A | . | R | S | . | I | A | H | N | . | D | T | . | A | H | . | I | D | S | L | . | O | T | S | H | . | R |
| E | E | B | E | . | . | O | D | T | A | . | U | E | G | R | H | A | T | . | E | D | R | N | S | A | . | . | W |
| R | I | E | T | T | H | T | . | U | T | B | H | . | E | L | . | E | U | I | N | N | F | A | O | H | R | T | T |
| A | U | N | N | . | A | R | T | O | E | F | . | . | L | D | I | E | F | T | E | N | . | I | O | R | F | P | . |
| . | E | N | D | O | G | D | A | N | R | O | . | L | S | . | O | E | N | D | N | I | E | S | . | – | A | E | N |
| K | D | C | . | N | H | A | E | B | I | . | R | E | E | H | . | T | T | . | O | N | . | O | T | . | H | E | E |
| B | . | A | E | O | A | L | R | G | L | . | E | E | . | H | O | T | F | . | . | T | G | A | L | . | O | Y | S |
| L | T | L | E | A | R | U | . | S | A | U | N | . | D | G | . | N | H | I | I | Y | S | A | . | L | S | P | U |
| . | L | S | L | T | E | N | N | A | . | V | A | R | N | E | D | S | . | . | A | S | S | E | S | I | U | T | M |
| S | E | E | D | I | . | A | H | M | U | . | M | S | O | I | R | H | . | . | O | Y | F | B | . | . | T | S | O |
| E | M | Y | . | A | O | D | F | I | . | L | B | L | E | O | D | H | L | . | A | S | M | A | : | M | A | T | S |
| S | . | I | I | R | T | H | . | C | W | . | A | N | S | I | . | . | P | T | L | H | A | G | Y | I | E | N | D |
| . | . | S | B | N | E | A | F | H | O | P | R | E | E | T | . | S | T | . | H | S | E | . | . | N | K | O | I |
| P | N | U | G | . | S | L | . | L | M | A | A | H | I | E | E | T | S | I | T | H | I | W | E | . | . | T | A |
| A | T | . | . | E | W | I | H | T | I | S | T | E | E | I | H | A | A | M | L | . | L | S | . | G | U | N | P |
| I | O | K | N | . | . | E | S | H | . | T | S | . | T | E | E | R | P | O | H | F | A | E | N | B | S | . | . |
| D | N | E | I | Y | G | A | H | L | T | P | . | . | I | S | N | A | . | W | C | . | H | T | R | I | I | . | S |
| S | T | A | M | : | A | M | S | A | . | L | H | D | O | E | L | B | L | . | I | F | D | O | A | . | Y | M | E |
| O | S | T | . | . | B | F | Y | O | . | . | H | R | I | O | S | M | . | U | M | H | A | . | I | D | E | E | S |
| M | T | U | I | S | E | S | S | A | . | . | S | D | E | N | R | A | V | . | A | N | N | E | T | L | S | L | . |
| U | P | S | L | . | A | S | Y | I | I | H | N | . | G | D | . | N | U | A | S | . | U | R | A | E | L | T | L |
| S | Y | O | . | L | A | G | T | . | . | F | T | O | H | . | E | E | . | L | G | R | L | A | O | E | A | . | B |
| E | E | H | . | T | O | . | N | O | . | T | T | . | H | E | E | R | . | I | B | E | A | H | N | . | C | D | K |
| N | E | A | – | . | S | E | I | N | D | N | E | O | . | S | L | . | O | R | N | A | D | G | O | D | N | E | . |
| . | P | F | R | O | I | . | N | E | T | F | E | I | D | L | . | . | F | E | O | T | R | A | . | N | N | U | A |
| T | T | R | H | O | A | F | N | N | I | U | E | . | L | E | . | H | B | T | U | . | T | H | T | T | E | I | R |
| W | . | . | A | S | N | R | D | E | . | T | A | H | R | G | E | U | . | A | T | D | O | . | . | E | B | E | E |
| R | . | H | S | T | O | . | L | S | D | I | . | H | A | . | T | D | . | N | H | A | I | . | S | R | . | A | S |
| E | H | L | O | . | P | G | . | N | I | I | N | K | . | . | P | F | A | O | U | . | L | H | S | T | . | A | C |
| E | H | D | U | . | R | D | C | N | H | A | – | . | Y | E | A | F | R | I | D | L | . | . | A | E | T | H | . |
| T | T | . | H | F | E | O | . | . | S | E | I | I | G | R | N | O | E | T | . | S | O | I | F | H | . | . | T |
| E | H | L | E | C | . | I | P | N | I | O | D | R | E | H | . | C | B | . | U | E | L | U | L | R | . | T | N |
| . | E | S | E | I | R | H | E | : | . | E | S | R | T | A | . | E | A | P | U | S | S | – | T | K | I | A | N |
| H | S | S | . | . | G | M | A | A | T | I | E | L | . | L | I | I | 6 | W | O | . | 8 | M | . | + | + | + | + |

*Figure 43*

THE

Tragedie of King Ri-
chard the ſe-
cond.

*As it hath beene publikely acted
by the right Honourable the
Lorde Chamberlaine his Seruants.*

LONDON
Printed by Valentine Simmes for Androw Wiſe, and
are to be ſold at his ſhop in Paules church yard at
the ſigne of the Angel.
1597.

Fig. 44 *Richard the Second,* first quarto, and concealment.

## *Richard the Second*

| + | + | + | + | + | + | T | 7 | H | 9 | E | 5 | . | I | T | . | R | L | A | E | G | G | E | N |
|---|---|---|---|---|---|---|---|---|---|---|---|---|---|---|---|---|---|---|---|---|---|---|---|
| D | A | I | . | E | E | . | H | O | T | F | . | . | F | K | O | I | . | N | E | G | N | . | G |
| R | I | I | S | – | . | C | E | H | H | A | T | R | . | D | T | . | A | T | . | H | D | E | R |
| . | A | S | Y | E | . | – | H | C | C | O | R | N | U | D | H | . | C | A | . | S | S | . | E |
| I | L | T | U | . | A | H | P | A | . | T | N | H | I | . | . | B | P | E | O | E | H | N | S |
| E | . | . | S | P | I | U | H | B | . | L | T | I | A | K | . | E | D | L | L | Y | O | . | S |
| A | . | C | E | T | B | E | . | D | O | . | T | B | . | Y | E | . | R | T | A | H | . | E | D |
| . | N | R | A | I | . | G | E | H | S | T | I | . | W | H | . | O | W | N | O | O | R | U | D |
| R | N | A | A | B | . | L | R | E | O | . | F | T | . | H | S | E | E | . | M | L | M | O | I |
| R | S | D | . | E | E | . | N | C | I | H | T | A | N | M | E | B | L | E | A | R | V | L | . |
| A | Y | I | B | N | . | E | D | . | E | H | T | I | N | S | I | . | R | S | P | E | . | R | N |
| – | O | V | D | A | N | N | O | T | L | S | . | . | S | L | T | O | N | N | A | D | V | O | – |
| N | R | . | E | P | S | R | . | I | S | N | I | T | H | E | . | D | E | . | N | B | I | Y | A |
| . | L | V | R | A | E | L | B | E | M | N | A | T | H | I | C | N | . | E | E | . | D | S | R |
| I | O | M | L | M | . | E | E | S | H | . | T | F | . | O | E | R | L | . | B | A | A | N | R |
| D | U | R | O | O | N | W | O | . | H | W | . | I | T | S | H | E | G | . | I | À | R | N | . |
| D | E | . | H | A | T | R | . | E | Y | . | B | T | . | O | D | . | E | B | T | E | C | . | A |
| S | . | O | Y | L | L | D | E | . | K | A | I | T | L | . | B | H | U | I | P | S | . | . | E |
| S | N | H | E | O | E | P | B | . | . | I | H | N | T | . | A | P | H | A | . | U | T | L | I |
| E | . | S | S | . | A | C | . | H | D | U | N | R | O | C | C | H | – | . | E | Y | S | A | . |
| R | E | D | H | . | T | A | . | T | D | . | R | T | A | H | H | E | C | . | – | S | I | I | R |
| G | . | N | G | E | N | . | I | O | K | F | . | . | F | T | O | H | . | E | E | . | I | A | D |
| N | E | G | G | E | A | L | R | . | T | I | . | 5 | E | 9 | H | 7 | T | + | + | + | + | + | + |

*Figure 44*

THE
Hiſtorie of Troylus
and Creſſeida.

*As it was acted by the Kings Maieſties*
ſeruants at the Globe.

*Written by* William Shakeſpeare.

LONDON
Imprinted by *G.Eld* for *R. Bonian* and *H. Walley*, and
are to be ſold at the ſpred Eagle in Paules
Church-yeard, ouer againſt the
great North doore.
1609.

Fig. 45 *Troylus and Cresseida,* first quarto, and concealment.

THE
Tragœdy of Othello,
The Moore of Venice.

*As it hath beene diuerſe times acted at the*
Globe, and at the Black-Friers, by
*his Maieſties Seruants.*

*Written by* VVilliam Shakeſpeare.

*LONDON,*
ted by *N. O.* for *Thomas Walkley*, and are to be ſold at his
ſhop, at the Eagle and Child, in Brittans Burſſe.
1622.

Fig. 46 *Othello,* first quarto, and concealment.

## *Hamlet*

| + | + | + | + | + | + | + | + | + | + | + | + | 3 | T | O | H | 6 | E | I | . | . | T | L | R | L | A | E | G | D | I | N | C | U | A | R | L | T | L | . | . |
|---|---|---|---|---|---|---|---|---|---|---|---|---|---|---|---|---|---|---|---|---|---|---|---|---|---|---|---|---|---|---|---|---|---|---|---|---|---|---|---|
| N | H | H | I | O | S | J | T | . | O | D | R | N | I | A | E | . | . | L | O | . | F | N | . | . | H | R | A | O | M | F | L | . | E | D | T | E | . | T | P |
| N | R | I | I | R | N | P | C | . | E | N | . | O | O | D | F | N | . | O | D | L | E | . | N | T | M | A | A | . | R | L | K | . | E | N | . | . | B | E | Y |
| R | . | E | W | H | I | W | L | – | L | E | I | S | A | L | M | E | . | . | S | D | H | N | A | A | K | . | E | D | – | R | S | O | P | F | E | X | A | O | R |
| . | E | D | . | N | A | A | S | . | . | E | I | G | T | D | . | I | H | R | A | B | T | M | H | A | . | C | B | . | E | F | E | O | N | . | E | S | . | E | D |
| I | I | T | V | I | E | S | R | R | S | E | E | V | . | I | T | N | I | – | M | U | E | . | S | O | . | W | A | T | C | . | T | E | E | H | D | T | . | . | B |
| N | Y | I | . | . | H | O | I | S | S | L | . | A | H | . | I | S | G | A | H | : | N | N | E | O | S | D | S | N | E | O | . | L | S | . | E | F | R | O | – |
| . | V | E | A | I | N | T | T | T | S | I | . | C | I | . | N | E | . | H | T | T | H | . | E | N | . | I | C | . | I | S | T | T | T | N | I | A | E | V | . |
| – | O | R | F | E | . | S | L | . | O | E | N | S | D | S | O | E | N | N | : | H | A | G | S | I | . | H | A | . | L | S | S | I | O | H | . | . | I | Y | N |
| B | . | . | T | D | H | E | E | T | . | C | T | A | W | . | O | S | . | E | U | M | – | I | N | T | I | . | V | E | E | S | R | R | S | E | I | V | T | I | I |
| D | E | . | S | E | . | N | O | E | F | E | . | B | C | . | A | H | M | T | B | A | R | H | I | . | D | T | G | I | E | . | . | S | A | A | N | . | D | E | . |
| R | O | A | X | E | F | P | O | S | R | – | D | E | . | K | A | A | N | H | D | S | . | . | E | M | L | A | S | I | E | L | – | L | W | I | H | W | E | . | R |
| Y | E | B | . | . | N | E | . | K | L | R | . | A | A | M | T | N | . | E | L | D | O | . | N | F | D | O | O | . | N | E | . | C | P | N | R | I | I | R | N |
| P | T | . | E | T | D | E | . | L | F | M | O | A | R | H | . | . | N | F | . | O | L | . | . | E | A | I | N | R | D | O | . | T | J | S | O | I | H | H | N |
| . | . | L | T | L | R | A | U | C | N | I | D | G | E | A | L | R | L | T | . | . | I | E | 6 | H | O | T | 3 | + | + | + | + | + | + | + | + | + | + | + | + |

*Figure 47*

## HAMLET

This title page contained 230 letters, eleven punctuation marks and four digits in the date, which was used in this case, but not the period after it. Applying the 'front-back' method to this text one finds Poet. Fr.-Bacon, or it can be read Poet. Fr-.ancis. The chart begins and ends with six crosses, denoting empty spaces.

Fig. 48 *Much Adoe About Nothing,* first quarto, and concealment.

# Much adoe about Nothing.

*As it hath been sundrie times publikely* acted by the right honourable, the Lord Chamberlaine his seruants.

*Written by William Shakespeare.*

LONDON
Printed by V.S. for Andrew Wise, and William Aspley.
1600.

## *Much Adoe About Nothing*

| + | + | + | + | + | + | . | M | O | U | O | C | 6 | H | I | . | . | A | Y | D | E | O | L | E | P | . | S | A | A | B | . | O | M | U | A | T | I | . |
|---|---|---|---|---|---|---|---|---|---|---|---|---|---|---|---|---|---|---|---|---|---|---|---|---|---|---|---|---|---|---|---|---|---|---|---|---|---|
| L | N | L | O | I | T | W | H | . | I | D | N | N | G | A | . | . | A | E | S | S | . | I | I | W | T | . | . | W | H | E | A | R | T | D | H | N | . |
| A | B | . | E | R | E | O | N | F | . | . | S | S | U | . | N | V | D | . | R | Y | I | B | E | . | . | D | T | E | I | T | M | N | E | I | S | R | . |
| P | P | . | U | N | B | O | L | D | I | N | K | O | E | L | L | . | Y | E | . | R | A | A | C | E | T | P | E | S | D | E | . | K | B | A | Y | H | . |
| S | T | . | H | M | E | A | . | I | R | L | I | L | G | I | H | W | T | . | . | Y | H | B | O | . | N | N | O | E | U | T | R | T | A | I | B | R | L |
| W | E | . | . | S | T | T | H | N | E | A | . | V | L | R | O | E | R | S | D | . | . | S | C | I | H | H | A | . | M | E | B | N | E | I | R | A | L |
| L | A | R | I | E | N | B | E | M | . | A | H | H | I | C | S | . | . | D | S | R | E | O | R | L | V | . | A | E | N | H | T | T | S | . | . | E | W |
| L | R | B | I | A | T | R | T | U | E | O | N | N | . | O | B | H | Y | . | . | T | W | H | I | G | L | I | L | R | I | . | A | E | M | H | . | T | S |
| . | H | Y | A | B | K | . | E | D | S | E | P | T | E | C | A | A | R | . | E | Y | . | L | L | E | O | K | N | I | D | L | O | B | N | U | . | P | P |
| . | R | S | I | E | N | M | T | I | E | T | D | . | . | E | B | I | Y | R | . | D | V | N | . | U | S | S | . | . | F | N | O | E | R | E | . | B | A |
| . | N | H | D | T | R | A | E | H | W | . | . | T | W | I | I | . | S | S | E | A | . | . | A | G | N | N | D | I | . | H | W | T | I | O | L | N | L |
| . | I | T | A | U | M | O | . | B | A | A | S | . | P | E | L | O | E | D | Y | A | . | . | I | H | 6 | C | O | U | O | M | . | + | + | + | + | + | + |

*Figure 48*

### Much ado about Nothing

The text contains fewer letters than most title pages, 181, seven punctuation marks and four digits for the date. The date was used and the period after it also. This keeps the chart in balance, so that it begins and ends with three empty spaces, indicated by crosses. One finds a concealed BACO.N with word POET above the N.

A

Moſt pleaſaunt and excellent conceited Co-medie, of Syr *Iohn Falſtaffe*, and the merrie Wiues of *Windſor*.

Entermixed with ſundrie variable and pleaſing humors, of Syr *Hugh* the Welch Knight, Iuſtice *Shallow*, and his wiſe Couſin M. *Slender*.

With the ſwaggering vaine of Auncient *Piſtoll*, and Corporall *Nym*.

By *William Shakeſpeare*.

As it hath bene diuers times Acted by the right Honorable my Lord Chamberlaines ſeruants. Both before her Maieſtie, and elſe-where.

LONDON
Printed by T. C. for Arthur Iohnſon, and are to be ſold at his ſhop in Powles Church yard, at the ſigne of the Flower de Leuſe and the Crowne.
1602.

Fig. 49 *Merrie Wives of Windsor*, first quarto and concealment.

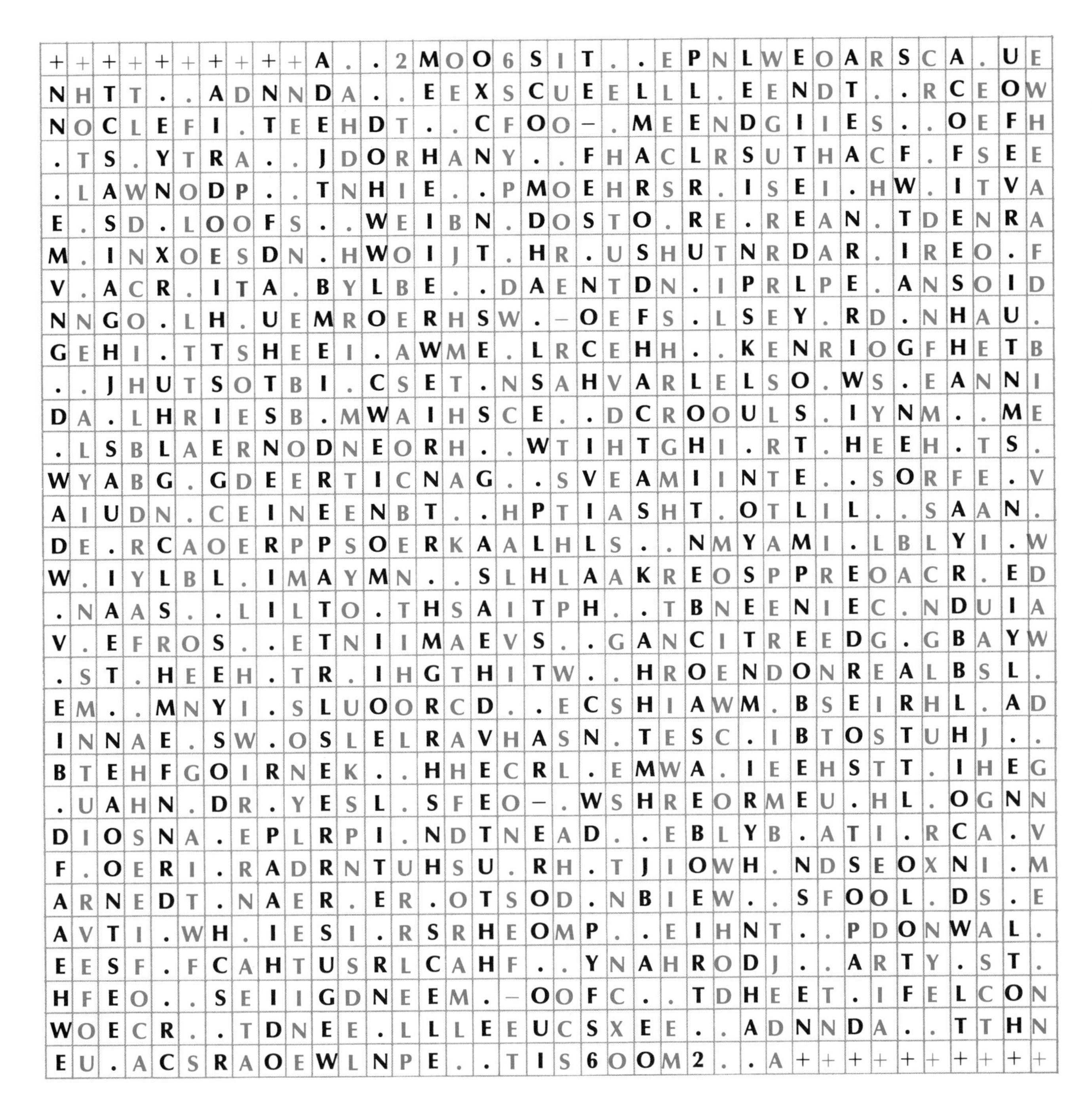

*Merrie Wives of Windsor*

*Figure 49*

The most excellent
Historie of the *Merchant of Venice.*

VVith the extreame crueltie of *Shylocke* the Iewe towards the sayd Merchant, in cutting a iust pound of his flesh: and the obtayning of *Portia* by the choyse of three chests.

*As it hath beene diuers times acted by the Lord Chamberlaine his Seruants.*

Written by William Shakespeare.

AT LONDON,
Printed by *I. R.* for Thomas Heyes,
and are to be sold in Paules Church-yard, at the signe of the Greene Dragon.
1600.

Fig. 50 *Merchant of Venice,* first quarto and concealment.

## *Merchant of Venice*

| + | + | + | + | + | + | + | + | . | T | O | H | O | E | 6 | . | I | M | . | O | N | S | O | T | G | . | A | E | R | X | D | C | . | E |
|---|---|---|---|---|---|---|---|---|---|---|---|---|---|---|---|---|---|---|---|---|---|---|---|---|---|---|---|---|---|---|---|---|---|
| E | L | N | L | E | E | E | N | R | T | G | . | . | H | E | I | H | S | T | T | . | O | F | R | O | I | . | E | E | . | N | O | G | F |
| I | . | S | T | . | H | E | E | H | . | T | M | . | E | T | R | A | C | . | H | D | A | R | N | A | T | Y | . | – | O | H | F | C | . |
| R | V | U | E | H | N | C | I | . | C | S | E | E | . | L | V | U | V | A | I | P | T | . | H | N | . | I | T | . | H | D | E | L | . |
| O | E | S | X | . | T | E | R | B | E | . | A | O | M | T | E | . | . | E | C | R | R | A | U | . | E | D | L | N | T | A | I | . | E |
| S | . | E | O | Y | F | E | . | H | S | . | H | S | Y | A | L | M | O | O | C | H | K | T | E | . | . | R | T | O | H | F | E | . | . |
| R | J | . | E | I | W | . | E | Y | . | B | T | . | O | D | W | E | A | T | R | N | D | I | S | R | . | P | T | . | H | N | E | O | . |
| D | S | N | A | O | Y | L | D | . | . | T | M | A | E | . | R | E | C | R | H | A | A | E | N | P | T | S | . | E | I | K | N | A | . |
| H | C | S | U | . | T | M | T | A | I | I | N | L | G | L | . | I | A | W | . | . | J | Y | U | B | S | . | T | N | . | E | P | T | O |
| T | U | I | N | R | D | W | . | . | O | S | F | T | . | N | H | A | I | V | S | R | . | E | F | S | L | . | E | S | S | I | H | H | : |
| . | A | E | N | N | D | I | . | A | T | L | H | R | E | E | . | B | O | M | B | A | T | H | A | C | Y | . | N | D | I | R | N | O | G |
| L | . | . | O | E | F | H | . | T | P | . | O | Y | R | B | T | . | I | D | A | E | . | T | B | C | Y | A | . | . | T | S | H | E | E |
| M | . | I | C | T | H | . | O | S | Y | R | S | E | E | V | . | I | O | D | F | . | . | E | T | N | H | E | R | E | E | B | E | . | . |
| H | C | T | H | A | E | H | S | . | T | T | S | I | . | . | A | S | S | A | . | . | I | S | T | T | . | S | H | E | A | H | T | C | H |
| . | . | E | B | E | E | R | E | H | N | T | E | . | . | F | D | O | I | . | V | E | E | S | R | Y | S | O | . | H | T | C | I | . | M |
| E | E | H | S | T | . | . | A | Y | C | B | T | . | E | A | D | I | . | T | B | R | Y | O | . | P | T | . | H | F | E | O | . | . | L |
| G | O | N | R | I | D | N | . | Y | C | A | H | T | A | B | M | O | B | . | E | E | R | H | L | T | A | . | I | D | N | N | E | A | . |
| : | H | H | I | S | S | E | . | L | S | F | E | . | R | S | V | I | A | H | N | . | T | F | S | O | . | . | W | D | R | N | I | U | T |
| O | T | P | E | . | N | T | . | S | B | U | Y | J | . | . | W | A | I | . | L | G | L | N | I | I | A | T | M | T | . | U | S | C | H |
| . | A | N | K | I | E | . | S | T | P | N | E | A | A | H | R | C | E | R | . | E | A | M | T | . | . | D | L | Y | O | A | N | S | D |
| . | O | E | N | H | . | T | P | . | R | S | I | D | N | R | T | A | E | W | D | O | . | T | B | . | Y | E | . | W | I | E | . | J | R |
| . | . | E | F | H | O | T | R | . | . | E | T | K | H | C | O | O | M | L | A | Y | S | H | . | S | H | . | E | F | Y | O | E | . | S |
| E | . | I | A | T | N | L | D | E | . | U | A | R | R | C | E | . | . | E | T | M | O | A | . | E | B | R | E | T | . | X | S | E | O |
| . | L | E | D | H | . | T | I | . | N | H | . | T | P | I | A | V | U | V | L | . | E | E | S | C | . | I | C | N | H | E | U | V | R |
| . | C | F | H | O | – | . | Y | T | A | N | R | A | D | H | . | C | A | R | T | E | . | M | T | . | H | E | E | H | . | T | S | . | I |
| F | G | O | N | . | E | E | . | I | O | R | F | O | . | T | T | S | H | I | E | H | . | . | G | T | R | N | E | E | E | L | N | L | E |
| E | . | C | D | X | R | E | A | . | G | T | O | S | N | O | . | M | I | . | 6 | E | O | H | O | T | . | + | + | + | + | + | + | + | + |

*Figure 50*

# TO THE RIGHT HONOVRABLE, HENRY VVriothesley, Earle of Southhampton, and Baron of Titchfield.

HE loue I dedicate to your Lordship is without end: wherof this Pamphlet without beginning is but a superfluous Moity. The warrant I haue of your Honourable disposition, not the worth of my vntutord Lines makes it assured of acceptance. VVhat I haue done is yours, what I haue to doe is yours, being part in all I haue, deuoted yours. VVere my worth greater, my duety would shew greater, meane time, as it is, it is bound to your Lordship; To whom I wish long life still lengthned with all happinesse.

Your Lordships in all duety.

William Shakespeare.

A 2

Fig. 51 Dedication to *Lucrece,* first quarto and concealment.

# TO THE RIGHT HONORABLE
## Henrie VVriotheſley, Earle of Southampton, and Baron of Titchfield.

*Right Honourable, I know not how I ſhall offend in dedicating my vnpoliſht lines to your Lordſhip, nor how the worlde vvill cenſure mee for chooſing ſo ſtrong a proppe to ſupport ſo vveake a burthen, onelye if your Honour ſeeme but pleaſed, I account my ſelfe highly praiſed, and vowe to take aduantage of all idle houres, till I haue honoured you vvith ſome grauer labour. But if the firſt heire of my inuention proue deformed, I ſhall be ſorie it had ſo noble a god-father: and neuer after eare ſo barren a land, for feare it yeeld me ſtill ſo bad a harueſt, I leaue it to your Honourable ſuruey, and your Honor to your hearts content vvhich I wiſh may alvvaies anſvvere your ovvne vviſh, and the vvorlds hopefull expectation.*

Your Honors in all dutie,

William Shakeſpeare.

Fig. 52 Dedication to *Venus and Adonis,* first quarto and concealment.

# A Midſommer nights dreame.

As it hath beene ſundry times pub-
*lickely acted, by the Right honoura-*
ble, the Lord Chamberlaine his
*ſeruants.*

*Written by William Shakeſpeare.*

¶ Imprinted at London, for *Thomas Fiſher*, and are to
be ſoulde at his ſhoppe, at the Signe of the White Hart,
in *Fleeteſtreete.* 1600.

Fig. 53 *A Midsommer Night's Dreame,* first quarto, and concealment.

*A Midsommer Night's Dreame*

**See footnote 3, Chapter one, page 129.**

\+ A . M I D S O M M E R . N I G H T S . D R

E A M E . A S . I T . H A T H . B E E N E .

S U N D R Y . T I M E S . P U B – L I C K E

L Y . A C T E D . B Y . T H E . R I G H T .

H O N O U R A – B L E . T H E . L O R D . C

H A M B E R L A I N E . H I S . S E R V A N

T S . W R I T T E N . B Y . W I L L I A M .

S H A K E S P E A R E . M O T O S . S O L E

O . C O M P O N E R T . F L U C T U S . A L

C I O N E . 9 . I M P R I N T E D T . L O N

D O N . F O R . T H O M A S . F I S H E R .

A N D . A R E . T O . B E . S O U L D E . A

T . I S . S H O P P E . A T . T H E . S I G

N E . O F . T H E . W H I T E . H A R T . I

N . F L E E T E S T R E E T E . 1 6 0 0 . +

*Figure 53*

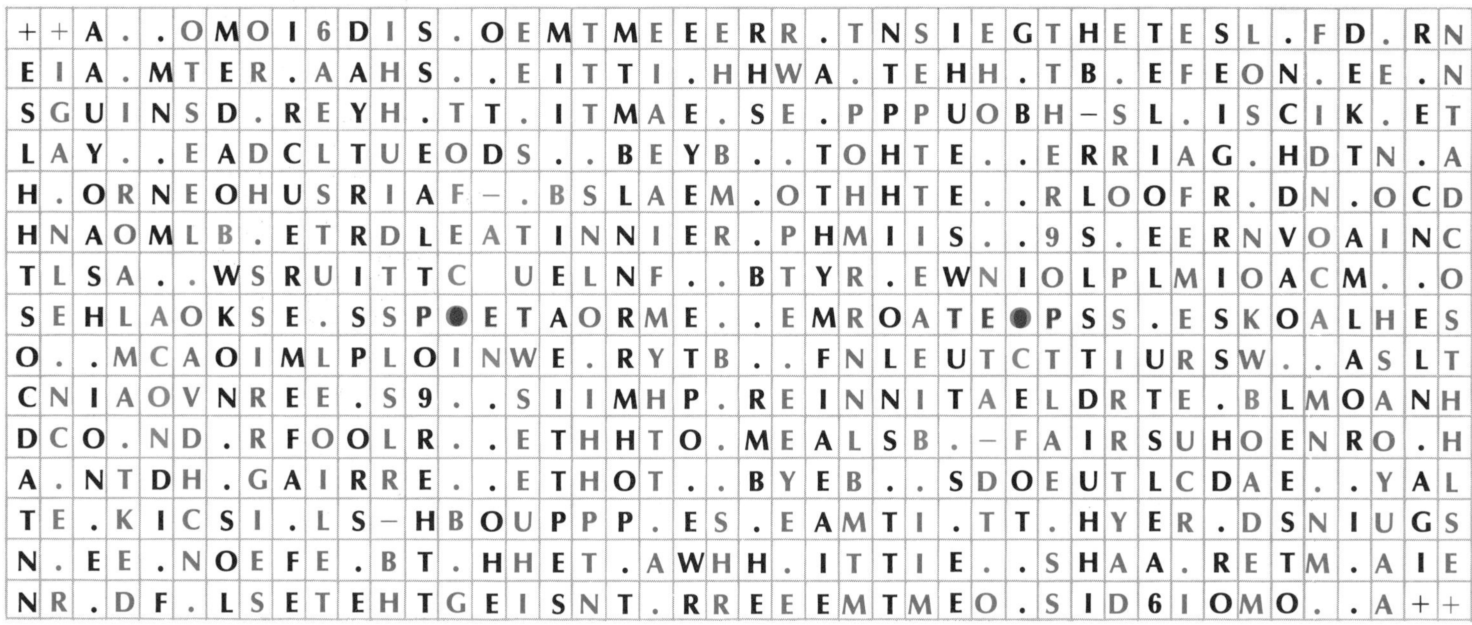

\+ + A . . O M O I 6 D I S . O E M T M E E R R . T N S I E G T H E T E S L . F D . R N

E I A . M T E R . A A H S . . E I T T I . H H W A . T E H H . T B . E F E O N . E E . N

S G U I N S D . R E Y H . T T . I T M A E . S E . P P P U O B H – S L . I S C I K . E T

L A Y . . E A D C L T U E O D S . . B E Y B . . T O H T E . . E R R I A G . H D T N . A

H . O R N E O H U S R I A F – . B S L A E M . O T H H T E . . R L O O F R . D N . O C D

H N A O M L B . E T R D L E A T I N N I E R . P H M I I S . . 9 S . E E R N V O A I N C

T L S A . . W S R U I T T C U E L N F . . B T Y R . E W N I O L P L M I O A C M . . O

S E H L A O K S E . S S P ● E T A O R M E . . E M R O A T E ● P S S . E S K O A L H E S

O . . M C A O I M L P L O I N W E . R Y T B . . F N L E U T C T T I U R S W . . A S L T

C N I A O V N R E E . S 9 . . S I I M H P . R E I N N I T A E L D R T E . B L M O A N H

D C O . N D . R F O O L R . . E T H H T O . M E A L S B . – F A I R S U H O E N R O . H

A . N T D H . G A I R R E . . E T H O T . . B Y E B . . S D O E U T L C D A E . . Y A L

T E . K I C S I . L S – H B O U P P P . E S . E A M T I . T T . H Y E R . D S N I U G S

N . E E . N O E F E . B T . H H E T . A W H H . I T T I E . . S H A A . R E T M . A I E

N R . D F . L S E T E H T G E I S N T . R R E E E M T M E O . S I D 6 I O M O . . A + +

A

# PLEASANT

Conceited Comedie

CALLED,

## Loues labors loſt.

As it vvas preſented before her Highnes
this laſt Chriſtmas.

Newly corrected and augmented
*By W. Shakeſpere.*

Imprinted at London by *W.W.*
for *Cutbert Burby.*
1598.

Fig. 54 *Loves Labors Lost,* first quarto, and concealment.

## *Loves Labors Lost*

| A | . | . | 8 | P | 9 | L | 5 | E | I | A | . | S | Y | A | B | N | R | T | U | . | B | C | . | O | T | N | R |
|---|---|---|---|---|---|---|---|---|---|---|---|---|---|---|---|---|---|---|---|---|---|---|---|---|---|---|---|
| C | E | E | B | I | T | T | U | E | C | D | . | . | R | C | O | O | F | M | . | E | W | D | . | I | W | E | . |
| . | Y | C | B | A | . | L | N | L | O | E | D | D | N | . | O | L | L | O | . | V | T | E | A | S | . | . | D |
| L | E | A | T | B | N | O | I | R | R | S | P | . | M | L | I | O | . | S | E | T | R | . | E | A | P | S | S |
| . | E | I | K | T | A | . | H | V | S | V | . | A | W | S | . | . | Y | P | B | R | . | E | D | S | E | E | T |
| N | N | T | E | E | M | D | G | . | U | B | A | E | . | F | D | O | N | R | A | E | . | . | D | H | E | E | T |
| R | C | . | E | H | R | I | R | G | O | H | C | N | . | E | Y | S | L | . | W | T | E | H | N | I | . | S | S |
| . | A | L | M | A | T | S | S | T | I | . | R | C | H | H | C | R | . | I | T | S | S | T | A | M | L | A | . |
| S | S | . | I | N | H | E | T | W | . | L | S | Y | E | . | N | C | H | O | G | R | I | R | H | E | . | C | R |
| T | E | E | H | D | . | . | E | A | R | N | O | D | F | . | E | A | B | U | . | G | D | M | E | E | T | N | N |
| T | E | E | S | D | E | . | R | B | P | Y | . | . | S | W | A | . | V | S | V | H | . | A | T | K | I | E | . |
| S | S | P | A | E | . | R | T | E | S | . | O | I | L | M | . | P | S | R | R | I | O | N | B | T | A | E | L |
| D | . | . | S | A | E | T | V | . | O | L | L | O | . | N | D | D | E | O | L | N | L | . | A | B | C | Y | . |
| . | E | W | I | . | D | W | E | . | M | F | O | O | C | R | . | . | D | C | E | U | T | T | I | B | E | E | C |
| R | N | T | O | . | C | B | . | U | T | R | N | B | A | Y | S | . | A | I | E | 5 | L | 9 | P | 8 | . | . | A |

*Figure 54*

THE

CRONICLE

History of Henry the fift,

With his battell fought at *Agin Court* in *France*. Togither with *Auntient Pistoll*.

*As it hath bene sundry times playd by the Right honorable the Lord Chamberlaine his seruants.*

LONDON

Printed by *Thomas Creede*, for Tho. Milling-ton, and Iohn Busby. And are to be sold at his house in Carter Lane, next the Powle head. 1600.

Fig. 55 *Henry V,* first quarto, and concealment.

## *Henry V*

| | | | | | | | | | | | | | | | | | | | | | | | | | | | | | | | | | | | |
|---|---|---|---|---|---|---|---|---|---|---|---|---|---|---|---|---|---|---|---|---|---|---|---|---|---|---|---|---|---|---|---|---|---|---|---|
| + | + | + | + | T | . | H | D | E | A | . | E | C | H | R | . | O | E | N | L | I | W | C | O | L | P | E | . | . | E | H | H | I | T | S | . |
| T | T | O | X | R | E | Y | N | . | . | O | E | F | N | . | A | H | L | E | . | N | R | R | E | Y | T | . | R | T | A | H | C | E | . | . | N |
| F | I | I | . | F | E | T | S | . | U | W | O | I | H | T | . | H | S | . | I | H | H | I | . | S | T | . | A | B | . | A | D | T | L | T | O |
| E | S | L | . | L | E | . | B | F | . | O | O | U | T | G | . | H | E | T | R | . | A | A | . | T | D | . | N | A | A | G | . | I | Y | N | B |
| . | S | C | U | O | B | U | . | R | N | T | H | . | O | I | J | N | . | . | D | F | N | R | A | A | . | N | N | C | O | E | T | . | – | T | G |
| O | N | G | I | I | L | T | L | H | I | E | M | R | . | . | O | W | H | I | T | T | . | H | R | . | O | A | F | U | . | N | E | T | D | I | E |
| E | E | N | R | T | C | . | . | P | S | I | A | S | M | T | O | O | H | L | T | L | . | . | Y | A | B | S | . | . | D | I | E | T | T | . | N |
| H | I | A | R | T | P | H | . | . | N | B | O | E | D | N | N | E | O | . | L | S | . | U | C | N | . | D | T | R | . | Y | S | . | A | T | T |
| I | I | M | R | E | E | S | V | . | . | P | E | L | R | A | E | Y | N | D | L | . | V | B | V | Y | . | . | T | T | I | H | S | E | S | . | E |
| R | R | I | I | G | V | H | . | T | S | . | T | H | N | O | A | N | V | O | R | R | E | A | S | B | . | L | S | E | I | . | H | T | . | H | E |
| E | N | . | I | L | A | O | L | R | R | D | E | . | B | C | M | H | A | A | H | M | C | B | . | E | D | R | R | L | O | A | L | I | . | N | E |
| E | H | . | T | H | . | I | E | S | L | . | B | S | A | E | R | R | O | V | N | A | O | N | H | T | . | S | T | . | H | V | G | I | I | R | R |
| E | . | S | E | S | H | I | T | T | . | . | Y | V | B | V | . | L | D | N | Y | E | A | R | L | E | P | . | . | V | S | E | E | R | M | I | I |
| T | T | A | . | S | Y | . | R | T | D | . | N | C | U | . | S | L | . | O | E | N | N | D | E | O | B | N | . | . | H | P | T | R | A | I | H |
| N | . | T | T | E | I | D | . | . | S | B | A | Y | . | . | L | T | L | H | O | O | T | M | S | A | I | S | P | . | . | C | T | R | N | E | E |
| E | I | D | T | E | N | . | U | F | A | O | . | R | H | . | T | T | I | H | W | O | . | . | R | M | E | I | H | L | T | L | I | I | G | N | O |
| G | T | – | . | T | E | O | C | N | N | . | A | A | R | N | F | D | . | . | N | J | I | O | . | H | T | N | R | . | U | B | O | U | C | S | . |
| B | N | Y | I | . | G | A | A | N | . | D | T | . | A | A | . | R | T | E | H | . | G | T | U | O | O | . | F | B | . | E | L | . | L | S | E |
| O | T | L | T | D | A | . | B | A | . | T | S | . | I | H | H | I | . | S | H | . | T | H | I | O | W | U | . | S | T | E | F | . | I | I | F |
| N | . | . | E | C | H | A | T | R | . | T | Y | E | R | R | N | . | E | L | H | A | . | N | F | E | O | . | . | N | Y | E | R | X | O | T | T |
| . | S | T | I | H | H | E | . | . | E | P | L | O | C | W | I | L | N | E | O | . | R | H | C | E | . | A | E | D | H | . | T | + | + | + | + |

*Figure 55*

AN
EXCELLENT
conceited Tragedie
OF
Romeo and Iuliet,

As it hath been often (with great applauſe)
plaid publiquely, by the right Honourable the L. of *Hunſdon*
his Seruants.

LONDON,
Printed by Iohn Danter.
1597

Fig. 56 *Romeo and Juliet,* first quarto, and concealment.

A
Pleaſant Conceited
Hiſtorie, called The taming
of a Shrew.

As it was ſundry times acted by the
*Right honorable the Earle of*
Pembrook his ſeruants.

Printed at London by Peter Short and
*are to be ſold by Cutbert Burbie, at his*
ſhop at the Royall Exchange.
1594.

Fig. 57 *The Taming of a Shrew,* first quarto, and concealment.

THE

# HISTORY OF HENRIE THE FOVRTH;

With the battell at Shrewsburie,
*betweene the King and Lord*
Henry Percy, ſurnamed
Henrie Hotſpur of
the North.

*With the humorous conceits of Sir*
Iohn Falſtalffe.

AT LONDON,
Printed by *P. S.* for *Andrew Wiſe*, dwelling
in Paules Churchyard, at the ſigne of
the Angell. 1598.

Fig. 58 *Henry IV*, part one, first quarto, and concealment.

THE

# Second part of Henrie the fourth, continuing to his death,

*and coronation of Henrie*
the fift.

With the humours of ſir Iohn Fal
*ſtaffe, and ſwaggering*
Piſtoll.

*As it hath been ſundrie times publikely*
acted by the right honourable, the Lord
Chamberlaine his ſeruants.

*Written by William Shakeſpeare.*

LONDON
Printed by V.S. for Andrew Wiſe, and
William Aſpley.
1600.

Fig. 59 *Henry IV*, part two, first quarto, and concealment.

THE

# Firſt part of the Con-

tention betwixt the two famous Houſes of Yorke
and Lancaſter, with the death of the good
Duke Humphrey:

And the baniſhment and death of the Duke of
*Suffolke*, and the Tragicall end of the proud Cardinall
of *VVincheſter*, vvith the notable Rebellion
of *Iacke Cade*:

*And the Duke of Yorkes firſt claime vnto the
Crowne.*

LONDON
Printed by Thomas Creed, for Thomas Millington,
and are to be ſold at his ſhop vnder Saint Peters
Church in Cornwall.
1594.

Fig. 60 *Henry VI,* part two, first quarto, and concealment.

*Henry VI, Part Two*

| + | + | + | + | + | + | + | + | + | + | + | + | + | + | T | 4 | H | 9 | E | 5 | . | I | F | . |
|---|---|---|---|---|---|---|---|---|---|---|---|---|---|---|---|---|---|---|---|---|---|---|---|
| I | L | R | L | S | A | T | W | . | N | P | R | A | O | R | C | T | . | . | N | O | I | F | . |
| . | H | T | C | H | R | E | U | . | H | C | C | O | . | N | S | = | R | T | E | E | T | N | E |
| T | P | I | . | O | T | N | N | . | I | B | A | E | S | T | . | W | R | I | E | X | D | T | N |
| . | U | T | . | H | P | E | O | . | H | T | S | W | . | O | S | . | I | F | H | A | . | M | T |
| O | A | U | . | S | D | . | L | H | O | O | S | U | . | S | E | E | B | S | . | . | O | O | T |
| F | . | . | E | Y | R | O | A | R | . | K | D | E | N | . | A | A | . | N | N | D | O | . | T |
| L | G | A | N | N | I | C | L | A | L | S | I | T | M | E | . | R | S | . | A | W | M | I | O |
| T | H | H | T | . | . | T | R | H | O | E | F | . | . | D | D | E | E | A | E | T | R | H | C |
| . | . | O | S | F | A | . | M | T | O | H | H | E | T | . | . | G | Y | O | B | O | . | D | D |
| . | E | D | T | U | N | K | I | E | R | . | P | H | . | U | N | M | O | P | D | H | N | R | O |
| E | L | Y | . | : | C | A | . | N | T | D | . | . | S | T | A | H | T | E | I | . | R | B | E |
| A | V | N | . | I | E | S | R | H | E | M | N | E | L | N | U | T | V | . | . | A | T | N | I |
| D | S | . | S | D | E | E | R | A | I | T | V | H | . | . | E | O | N | F | W | . | O | T | R |
| H | C | E | . | . | E | D | H | U | T | K | . | E | O | . | T | O | N | F | U | . | . | S | E |
| U | M | F | I | F | A | O | L | L | C | K | . | E | T | . | S | A | R | N | I | D | F | . | . |
| T | S | H | E | E | K | . | R | T | O | R | Y | A | . | G | F | I | O | C | . | A | E | L | K |
| L | U | . | D | E | . | N | E | D | H | . | T | O | . | F | D | . | N | T | A | H | : | E | E |
| . | D | P | A | R | C | O | . | U | E | D | K | . | C | C | A | A | J | R | . | D | F | I | O |
| N | . | A | N | L | O | L | I | . | L | O | L | F | E | . | B | V | E | V | R | I | . | N | E |
| C | L | H | B | E | A | S | T | T | O | E | N | R | . | . | E | V | H | V | T | I | . | T | H |
| H | T | . | I | T | V | H | V | E | . | . | R | N | E | O | T | T | S | A | E | B | H | L | C |
| E | N | . | I | R | V | E | V | B | . | E | F | L | O | L | . | I | L | O | L | N | A | . | N |
| O | I | F | D | . | R | J | A | A | C | C | . | K | D | E | U | . | O | C | R | A | P | D | . |
| E | E | : | H | A | T | N | . | D | F | . | O | T | . | H | D | E | N | . | E | D | . | U | L |
| K | L | E | A | . | C | O | I | F | G | . | A | Y | R | O | T | R | . | K | E | E | H | S | T |
| . | . | F | D | I | N | R | A | S | . | T | E | . | K | C | L | L | O | A | F | I | F | M | U |
| E | S | . | . | U | F | N | O | T | . | O | E | . | K | T | V | H | D | E | . | . | E | C | H |
| R | T | O | . | W | F | N | O | E | . | . | H | V | T | I | A | R | E | E | D | S | . | S | D |
| I | N | T | A | . | . | V | T | U | N | L | E | N | M | E | H | R | S | E | I | . | N | V | A |
| E | B | R | . | I | E | T | H | A | T | S | . | . | D | T | N | . | A | C | : | . | Y | L | E |
| O | R | N | H | D | P | O | M | N | U | . | H | P | . | R | E | I | K | N | U | T | D | E | . |
| D | D | . | O | B | O | Y | G | . | . | T | E | H | H | O | T | M | . | A | F | S | O | . | . |
| C | H | R | T | E | A | E | E | D | D | . | . | F | E | O | H | R | T | . | . | T | H | H | T |
| O | I | M | W | A | . | S | R | . | E | M | T | I | S | L | A | L | C | I | N | N | A | G | L |
| T | . | O | D | N | N | . | A | A | . | N | E | D | K | . | R | A | O | R | Y | E | . | . | F |
| T | O | O | . | . | S | B | E | E | S | . | U | S | O | O | H | L | . | D | S | . | U | A | O |
| T | M | . | A | H | F | I | . | S | O | . | W | S | T | H | . | O | E | P | H | . | T | U | . |
| N | T | D | X | E | I | R | W | . | T | S | E | A | B | I | . | N | N | T | O | . | I | P | T |
| E | N | T | E | E | T | R | = | S | N | . | O | C | C | H | . | U | E | R | H | C | T | H | . |
| . | F | I | O | N | . | . | T | C | R | O | A | R | P | N | . | W | T | A | S | L | R | L | I |
| . | F | I | . | 5 | E | 9 | H | 4 | T | + | + | + | + | + | + | + | + | + | + | + | + | + | + |

*Figure 60*

The true Tragedie of Richard
*Duke of Yorke, and the death of*
good King Henrie the Sixt,

*with the whole contention betweene*
the two Houſes Lancaſter
and Yorke, as it was ſundrie times
acted by the Right Honourable the Earle of Pem-
brooke his ſeruants.

Printed at London by P. S. for Thomas Milling-
*ton, and are to be ſold at his ſhoppe vnder*
*Saint Peters Church in*
*Cornwal.* 1595.

Fig. 61 *Henry VI,* part three, first quarto, and concealment.

# *Henry VI, Part Three*

| + | + | + | + | + | + | + | + | + | + | + | + | + | + | T | . | H | L | E | A | . | W | T | N | R | R | U | O | E | C | . | . | T | N | R | I | A | . | G | H | E | C | D | R | I | V | E | H |
|---|---|---|---|---|---|---|---|---|---|---|---|---|---|---|---|---|---|---|---|---|---|---|---|---|---|---|---|---|---|---|---|---|---|---|---|---|---|---|---|---|---|---|---|---|---|---|---|
| . | C | O | . | F | S | . | R | R | E | I | T | C | E | H | P | A | . | R | T | D | N | . | I | D | A | V | S | K | . | E | R | . | E | O | D | F | N | . | U | Y | . | O | E | R | P | K | P |
| E | O | . | H | A | S | N | . | D | S | . | I | T | H | H | . | E | T | . | A | D | . | E | D | A | L | T | O | H | S | . | . | O | E | F | B | . | . | G | O | O | T | O | . | D | E | . | R |
| K | A | I | . | N | D | G | N | . | A | H | . | E | N | N | O | R | T | I | – | E | G | . | N | T | I | H | L | E | L | . | I | S | M | I | . | X | S | T | A | . | M | W | O | I | H | T | T |
| H | . | . | R | T | O | H | F | E | . | . | S | W | . | H | P | O | . | L | Y | E | B | . | . | C | N | O | O | N | D | T | N | E | O | N | L | T | . | I | T | O | A | N | . | . | D | B | E |
| E | T | T | N | W | I | E | R | E | P | N | . | E | M | . | . | T | T | H | . | E | S | . | T | T | N | W | A | O | V | . | R | H | E | O | S | U | . | S | S | E | I | S | H | . | . | L | E |
| A | K | N | O | C | O | A | R | S | B | T | – | E | M | R | E | . | P | A | . | N | F | D | O | . | . | Y | E | O | L | R | R | K | A | E | E | . | . | A | E | S | H | . | T | I | . | T | E |
| . | L | W | B | A | – | S | A | . | R | S | U | U | O | N | N | D | O | R | H | I | . | E | T | . | H | T | G | I | I | M | R | E | . | S | E | . | H | A | T | C | . | T | Y | E | B | D | . |
| . | D | B | E | Y | T | . | C | T | A | H | . | E | S | . | E | R | M | I | I | G | T | H | . | T | E | . | I | H | R | O | D | N | N | O | U | U | S | R | . | A | S | – | A | B | W | L | . |
| E | T | . | I | T | . | H | S | E | A | . | . | E | E | A | K | R | R | L | O | E | Y | . | . | O | D | F | N | . | A | P | . | E | R | M | E | – | T | B | S | R | A | O | C | O | N | K | A |
| E | L | . | . | H | S | I | E | S | S | . | U | S | O | E | H | R | . | V | O | A | W | N | T | T | . | S | E | . | H | T | T | . | . | M | E | . | N | P | E | R | E | I | W | N | T | T | E |
| E | B | D | . | . | N | A | O | T | I | . | T | L | N | O | E | N | T | D | N | O | O | N | C | . | . | B | E | Y | L | . | O | P | H | . | W | S | . | . | E | F | H | O | T | R | . | . | H |
| T | T | H | I | O | W | M | . | A | T | S | X | . | I | M | S | I | . | L | E | L | H | I | T | N | . | G | E | – | I | T | R | O | N | N | E | . | H | A | . | N | G | D | N | . | I | A | K |
| R | . | E | D | . | O | T | O | O | G | . | . | B | F | E | O | . | . | S | H | O | T | L | A | D | E | . | D | A | . | T | E | . | H | H | T | I | . | S | D | . | N | S | A | H | . | O | E |
| P | K | P | R | E | O | . | Y | U | . | N | F | D | O | E | . | R | E | . | K | S | U | A | D | I | . | N | D | T | R | . | A | P | H | E | C | T | I | E | R | R | . | S | F | . | O | C | . |
| H | E | V | I | R | D | C | E | H | G | . | A | I | R | N | T | . | . | C | E | O | U | R | R | N | T | W | . | A | E | L | H | . | T | + | + | + | + | + | + | + | + | + | + | + | + | + | + |

*Figure 61*

THE<br>MOST LA-<br>mentable Romaine<br>Tragedie of Titus Andronicus:

As it was Plaide by the Right Ho-<br>nourable the Earle of *Darbie*, Earle of *Pembrooke*,<br>and Earle of *Suſſex* their Seruants.

LONDON,<br>Printed by Iohn Danter, and are<br>to be ſold by *Edward White* & *Thomas Millington*,<br>at the little North doore of Paules at the<br>ſigne of the Gunne,<br>1594.

Fig. 62 *Titus and Andronicus,* first quarto, and concealment.

## *Titus Andronicus*

| . | T | E | H | N | E | N | . | U | M | G | O | . | S | E | T | H | . | T | L | . | A | F | – | O | M | . | E | E | N | N | T | G | A | I | B | S | L | . | E |
|---|---|---|---|---|---|---|---|---|---|---|---|---|---|---|---|---|---|---|---|---|---|---|---|---|---|---|---|---|---|---|---|---|---|---|---|---|---|---|---|
| E | . | H | R | T | O | . | M | T | A | A | I | . | N | S | E | E | . | L | T | U | R | A | A | P | G | . | E | F | D | O | I | . | E | E | . | R | O | O | F |
| O | . | D | T | . | I | H | T | T | U | R | S | O | . | N | A | . | N | E | D | L | R | T | O | T | N | I | I | L | C | . | U | E | S | H | : | T | A | . | S |
| T | . | A | I | . | T | N | . | O | W | T | A | G | S | N | . | I | P | L | L | L | A | I | I | M | D | . | E | S | . | A | B | M | Y | O | . | H | T | T | H |
| & | E | E | . | T | R | I | I | H | G | W | H | . | T | D | . | R | H | A | O | W | – | D | N | E | O | . | U | Y | R | B | A | . | B | D | L | L | E | O | . |
| S | T | . | H | E | E | B | . | . | E | O | A | T | R | . | L | E | E | R | . | A | O | . | F | D | . | N | D | A | A | . | R | R | B | E | I | T | E | N | . |
| A | E | D | A | . | R | N | L | H | E | O | . | J | O | . | F | Y | . | B | P | . | E | D | M | E | B | T | R | N | O | I | O | R | K | P | E | . | . | N | A |
| O | N | D | D | N | . | O | E | L | A | . | R | M | L | A | E | U | . | Q | O | N | F | U | . | N | S | . | U | T | S | U | S | A | E | . | X | C | . | N | T |
| U | H | N | E | . | I | T | R | U | . | A | S | . | E | S | R | T | V | N | A | A | N | V | T | R | S | E | . | S | A | . | U | R | T | I | . | E | N | H | U |
| T | N | . | C | X | . | E | A | S | U | S | T | U | . | S | N | . | U | F | N | O | Q | . | U | E | A | L | M | R | . | A | L | E | O | . | N | D | D | N | O |
| A | N | . | . | E | P | K | R | O | I | O | N | R | T | B | E | M | D | E | . | P | B | . | Y | F | . | O | J | . | O | E | H | L | N | R | . | A | D | E | A |
| . | N | E | T | I | E | B | R | R | . | A | A | D | N | . | D | F | . | O | A | . | R | E | E | L | . | R | T | A | O | E | . | . | B | E | E | H | . | T | S |
| . | O | E | L | L | D | B | . | A | B | R | Y | U | . | O | E | N | D | – | W | O | A | H | R | . | D | T | . | H | W | G | H | I | I | R | T | . | E | E | & |
| H | T | T | H | . | O | Y | M | B | A | . | S | E | . | D | M | I | I | A | L | L | L | P | I | . | N | S | G | A | T | W | O | . | N | T | . | I | A | . | T |
| S | . | A | T | : | H | S | E | U | . | C | L | I | I | N | T | O | T | R | L | D | E | N | . | A | N | . | O | S | R | U | T | T | H | I | . | T | D | . | O |
| F | O | O | R | . | E | E | . | I | O | D | F | E | . | G | P | A | A | R | U | T | L | . | E | E | S | N | . | I | A | A | T | M | . | O | T | R | H | . | E |
| E | . | L | S | B | I | A | G | T | N | N | E | E | . | M | O | – | F | A | . | L | T | . | H | T | E | S | . | O | G | M | U | . | N | E | N | H | E | T | . |

*Figure 62*

# *FOOTNOTES*

Chapter One

[1] *Baconiana,* Vol. XVII, No. 65 (Third Series), London, June 1923.

[2] The following was written by Francis Bacon in his *De Augmentis,* as translated from the Latin by Gilbert Watts, 1640: "Wherefore let us come to cyphars. Their kinds are many, as Cyphars simple; cyphars of double letters under one character; Wheele cyphars; Kay cyphars; cyphars of words; Others. But the virtues of them whereby they are to be preferred are Three; That they be ready, and not laborous to write; That they be sure, and lie not open to Deciphering; And lastly, if it be possible, that they be managed without suspicion. But that jealousies may be taken away, we will annexe an other invention, which in truth, we devised in our youth, when at Paris; and is a thing that yet seemeth to us not worthy to be lost."

Then follows a detailed description of Bacon's biliteral cipher. He continues about ciphers in general:

"The Knowledge of Cyphering hath drawn on with it a Knowledge relative unto it, which is the knowledge of deseyphering, or of Descreting cyphers, though a man were utterly ignorant of the Alphabet of the Cypher, and the Capitulations of secrecy past between the parties. Certainly it is an Art which requires great paines and a good witt and is (as the other was) consecrate to the Counsels of Princes; yet not withinstanding by diligent prevision it may be made unprofitable, though, as things are, it be of great use. For if good and faithful Cyphers were invented & practised, many of them would delude and forestall all the cunning of the Decyphere, which yet are very apt and easie to be read or written, but the rawness and unskilflness of Secretaries, and clarks in the Courts of Princes, is such, that many times the greatest matters are committed to futile and weake Cyphers."

[3] How were the quartos 'strangely printed.' If you will look closely at the title pages of some of the quartos, as for example, 'A Midsummer Night's Dreame' (fig. 53) you will be

struck by peculiar things. For instance the word publickeley is divided by a hyphen but the first part of the word is in ordinary type and the part after the hyphen (as well as the rest of the line) is in italics. The last word honourable is divided with a hyphen after the 'a', and 'ble' on the next line NOT in italics. The word *imprinted,* (at the bottom) is followed by the letter 't' without an 'a' before it to make 'at' and the 'h' of 'his' has been messed up so that it reads "atis shoppe." The point is that this *is* strangely done for a title page, yet when it is faithfully put down in a line of 22 spaces with two crosses to begin the line and two crosses to end the last line to balance it then even the simple "frontwards" writing of the full text produces FRA BACON and POET (twice) and the 'double-it' text an other BACON from different words, etc. All this would not have appeared had I corrected the words and made it read "imprinted *at* London . . . to be soulde *at his* shoppe." In the case mentioned above of the hyphen in honourable being placed after the 'a' instead of after the 'r' here again in another similar case. For if the hyphen (which was needed at the end of the line) had been placed elsewhere the concealed name would not have appeared as it did in my work. Everything is calculated for this end. But it makes some of the title pages seem strangely printed. It seems to me that the alternation of italics and bold letters do not have any significance so far as the concealment is concerned. It is, however, hard to justify these two kinds of type and that is why I use the words strangely printed. Note also that I have used *all* the letters on the title page including "motos soleo componert fluctus ALCIONE" which appear in the picture.

4 Copyholds do not exist in the United States. In English law, the holding of land by right of being recorded as holder in the court of the manor, *Webster's International Dictionary.*

Chapter Two

1 Arte Maronem refers to Virgil because the full name of the great Latin poet was Publius Vergilus Maro (70-19 B.C.).

2 Published from the original manuscript by Mr. Rodd, 1838.

3 See note 2, Chapter 1.

Chapter Three

1 *Webster's International Dictionary* defines magistrate as "a person clothed with power in the executive government or some branch of it."

2 See article on Labeo in the *Encyclopaedia Britannica* (14th edition), which speaks of his mastery of jurisprudence, another similarity with Bacon's training in the law.

3 Venus was the god of love in the court of Jove.

4 From *Webster's International Dictionary.*

5 Melsome, p. 191.

6 Pallas Athene and her spear, as explained in a later chapter.

7 Startups refers to a high shoe of peasants or the buskins of tragedy that were used to increase the height of the actor.

8 Immerito, the Spanish word for the unknown.

9 The name of the stream which flowed from the Castalian spring of the Muses.

10 A high boot with heels worn by the ancient actors of tragedy.

11 From Castalia, a spring or fountain on Mt. Parnasas sacred to the Muses.

12 Allowance.

13 The great law school called the Inns of Court, consisted of the Inner Temple, Middle Temple, Lincoln's Inn and Gray's Inn. Percy Simpson in his *Notes of the Sequence of Shakespeare's Plays,* writes: — "John Manningham saw *Twelfth Night* at the Middle Temple on February 2, 1602; the Revels Accounts note court performances of *Othello* at Hallowmas (November 1), 1604, *Measure for Measure* on December 26, 1604 and *The Tempest* at Hallowmas, 1611."

Gray's Inn has existed as a School of Law since the 14th Century. The fine Elizabethan Hall, known as the Great Hall, was built in 1555-60 and contains a beautifully carved screen. Bacon retained his lodgings in Gray's Inn from 1576 till his death in 1626 a period of fifty years. A statue of him by Pomeroy (1912) stands in the South Garden.

Chapter Four

[1] Good dawning is used only twice in English literature, once in the *Promus* and once in *King Lear*.

[2] This proverb comes from the custom of hanging a bush (a sign) outside a tavern.

[3] Eagle, Roderick L., *Shakespeare: New Views for Old*. London, 1930.

Chapter Seven

[1] Anagrams were, as D'Israeli said, ..."then (in Elizabethan and Jacobean times) the fashionable amusements of the wittiest and most learned." Thus Galileo (1564-1642) announced his discovery that Venus had phases like the moon. He published a pamphlet containing the sentence: 'Haec immatura a me jam frustra leguntur-oy,' which is an anagram of 'Cynthia figuras amulatur Matur Amorum,' the object being apparently to protect his claim to priority during the period in which he would be making further observations, and before he was ready to make the full announcement. This also illustrates the awkward circumlocutions authors were driven to by the exigencies of the anagram. Galileo was obliged to designate Venus as 'The Mother of the Loves' and the moon by a Greek name 'Cynthiae,' and he has two letters left over, -oy, about the equivalent of 'hello.'

[2] Puerita means young one.

[3] *Discoveries*.

[4] By Cushman K. Davis, 1883.

[5] *Review of English Studies,* a quarterly, April-July 1943, p. 128.

Chapter Eight

[1] From the words on the title page on the Northumberland Manuscript. Modern spelling is "due."

[2] Bacon's home, Gorhambury, is on the site of the old Roman city of Verulam.

[3] The *Manes Verulamiani* were entered in the Stationers' Register "to Mistris Griffin and John Haviland" on 17th May, 1626. Bacon died on April 9th of that year. The edition was probably very limited. The copy in the British Museum is the only one recorded in the Bibliographical Society's Short Title Catalogue. There are, however, copies in Trinity College Library, Cambridge and the Libraries of Jesus College and All Souls, Oxford, and one in a private collection.

The Rev. William Sutton, S.J. of Dublin, translated all of the 32 eulogies that were gathered together by William Rawley, Bacon's chaplain in 1626. These were edited and published in 1950 by W.G.C. Gundry, of the Middle Temple, in a limited edition of 420 copies. Mr. Gundry's book contains Dr. Sutton's second and improved translations of the *Manes Verulamiani*.

Mr. Gundry, who is a Barrister-at-Law, gives his reason for publishing the book. He says, in the Introduction: —

"Our particular concern with the *Manes* is the light which they throw on Bacon's reputation as being:

1. A supreme poet, second to none.
2. The writer of unacknowledged literary work.
3. Associated with the theatre.
4. The center of a mystery which it was reserved for posterity to unravel

Edward Kennard Rand, classicist, of Harvard University, sponsored a translation into English prose of the *Manes Verulamiani* in 1904; this was printed for private circulation. Rand's translations are used where noted.

Dr. George Cantor of Halle and Wittenberg Universities published translations of all of the *Manes Verulamiani* in German in 1897 under the title: Die Rawley'sche Sammlung Von Zwei-und-dreissig Trauergedichten auf Francis Bacon.

[4] A native of Stagira, in ancient Macedonia, especially Aristotle.

# Bibliography


Bacon, Francis. The complete works of Francis Bacon was studied by the author in printed books and in original manuscript form as found in various British museums.

Baconiana, The Journal of the Francis Bacon Society, London, first published 1886. Various issues consulted.

Begley, The Rev. Walter (By A Cambridge Graduate). Is it Shakespeare. London, 1903.

Burgoyne, Frank. The Northumberland Manuscript, transcript with full facsimilie and notes. 1904.

Campbell, Lord John. Shakespeare's Legal Acquirements. London, 1859.

Dixon, William Hepworth. Personal History of Lord Bacon. Boston, 1861.

Dodd, Alfred. The Immortal Master. London, 19 .

Durning-Lawrence, Sir Edwin. Bacon is Shake-speare. New York, 1910.

Eagle, Roderick. Shakespeare: New Views for Old. London, 1930.

Encyclopaedia Britannica. Various editions. Chicago.

Heard, Franklin Fiske. Legal Acquirements of William Shakespeare. 1867. Shakespeare as a Lawyer. 1883.

Lewis, B. Roland. The Shakespeare Documents. 2 vols. Stanford, 1940-41.

Melsome, W.S. Bacon-Shakespeare Anatomy. Ed. by Roderick Eagle. London, 1945.

Pott, Mrs. Henry. The Promus of Formularies and Elegancies of Francis Bacon Illustrated and Elucidated by Passages from Shakespeare. London, 1883.

Reed, Edwin, Ed. Noteworthy Opinions. Boston, 1905.

Shakespeare, William. Complete Works. Various editions.

Spedding, James. Life and Letters of Francis Bacon. 7 vols. London, 1861-1874.

Webb, Judge Thomas. The Shakespeare Mystery. New York, 1902.

# *INDEX*